PRAISE
HACKING HO

Starr Sackstein and Connie Hamilton have assembled a book f
of great answers to the question, "How can we make hom
engaging and meaningful?" The "hacks" they offer are pract:
authentic and resonate for teachers at every grade level. Th
by-step directions move readers from theory to action. F
the advice in this book applies to in-school learning, to

DR. DOUG FISHER AND **DR. NANCY FREY**, PROF
AUTHOR'

Hacking Homework is a must read for teac.
not just another book advocating the elimination of homework—it
is a book in which the authors describe ten hacks/fixes that provide alternatives to traditional homework that make homework
about learning not compliance. All of the hacks provide sensible
and practical ways in which teachers—and parents—can support
learning outside school hours. I hope this book finds its way into
the professional library of every classroom teacher and that it is also
read carefully by administrators, policymakers and parents.

KEN O'CONNOR, EDUCATION CONSULTANT AND AUTHOR

Experienced educators Starr Sackstein and Connie Hamilton provide a wealth of practical ideas to help teachers reflect and improve
how they think about and implement homework practices. I can't
think of a better resource out there dealing with this issue, and it's
a challenging one for all of us in the classroom.

LARRY FERLAZZO, HIGH SCHOOL TEACHER AND AUTHOR

Sackstein and Hamilton provide a sound game plan to monumentally change learning cultures during and outside of the school day. Personal anecdotes from educators in the field provide a glimpse into the headaches of homework and how teachers can make learning relevant. This book will change your outlook on homework and improve your practice as an educator.

BRAD CURRIE, FOUNDING PARTNER OF EVOLVING EDUCATORS

A must read for all educators, *Hacking Homework* provides educators the insight they need to rethink the homework they are assigning. In addition, educators have applicable hacks to ensure they are moving their classrooms in the right direction. Educators have been having the homework debate for years; finally a book comes along that can move teachers in a direction of best practices that aligns with the research.

CRAIG VROOM, PRINCIPAL, HILLIARD WEAVER MIDDLE SCHOOL. HILLIARD CITY SCHOOL DISTRICT.

Starr and Connie believe that shaking up our homework policy is one of the best decisions they have ever made for kids. I agree! *Hacking Homework* shows how teachers and parents can take the stress out of homework and focus on what really matters. They emphasize why family time is simply too precious to continue the homework policy of handing out mundane assignments. *Hacking Homework* provides multiple alternatives to "homework" that bridge the gap between play and learning.

BARBARA BRAY, AUTHOR, CO-FOUNDER OF PERSONALIZE LEARNING, LLC, AND OWNER/FOUNDER OF MY ECOACH AND RETHINKING LEARNING

HACKING HOMEWORK

HACKING
HOMEWORK

10 Strategies That Inspire Learning
Outside the Classroom

Starr Sackstein
Connie Hamilton

PUBLICATIONS

These books are available at special discounts when purchased in quantity for use as premiums, promotions, fundraising, and educational use. For inquiries and details, contact us at www.hacklearning.org.

Published by Times 10
Cleveland, OH
HackLearning.org

Cover Design by Tracey Henterly
Interior Design by Steven Plummer
Editing by Sydney Reese
Proofreading by Jennifer Jas

Library of Congress Control Number: 2016950710

ISBN: 978-0-9861049-7-8
First Printing: October, 2016

CONTENTS

Dedication. 9

Publisher's Foreword 11

Introduction 15
It's time to reimagine homework

Hack 1: Break Up With Daily Homework. 23
Work around the policies

Hack 2: Teach Organization and Responsibility in Class. 37
Ramp up accountability, and time management skills

Hack 3: Cultivate Rapport. 55
Establish positive relationships to motivate learning

Hack 4: Customize to Meet Student Needs 71
Be flexible with assignments and timelines

Hack 5: Encourage Students to Play 85
Support innovation and creativity

Hack 6: Spark Curiosity Before the Lesson 101
Make connections that generate interest in learning

Hack 7: Use the Digital Playground 111
Harness social media for learning

Hack 8: Amplify Student Voice 127
Incorporate choice in how kids learn at home

Hack 9: Team Up With Families 141
Model instructional strategies for parents

Hack 10: Display Growth 157
Empower students to track their improvement and display progress

Conclusion 171
It's time to rethink how learning happens outside of school

Other Books in the *Hack Learning Series*. 175
Hack Learning Resources. 179
About the Authors. 181
Acknowledgements 183

DEDICATION

Connie: To my three children Trey, Luke, and Allie, for the sacrifices you made to allow me to make this book come to life. You have shown me what caring and loving young adults you are. To my favorite kid (you know which one you are), I love you and am proud you call me "mom." To my husband Paul for being my rock and encouraging me to reach my dreams. I couldn't have done this without your love and support.

Starr: To Logan, who has helped me understand the value of home time and how it mustn't be squandered doing meaningless worksheets. You have helped me reconsider what is necessary at home and because of our time, I work to value the time of my students' families. You remain the most constant source of inspiration in every area of my life. To my students and their families, thank you for your honest feedback and dialogue to improve learning in our shared spaces.

PUBLISHER'S FOREWORD

I MAY HAVE BEEN the biggest liar at Cleveland's Myron T. Herrick Junior High. At 12 years old, I hated school more than anyone but what I truly loathed was homework. Each night, my teachers distributed an endless stream of workbooks, worksheets, textbook chapters, and other horrible assignments—all far too tedious to describe in detail. I didn't understand how answering 25 math problems or summarizing the Battle of Antietam would serve me later in life, so in most cases I decided I just wouldn't do it.

Instead, I learned to lie about my homework. I crafted stories that the best detectives couldn't unravel. My skill at prevarication was unrivaled, and prompting teachers to forgive my missing homework was one of a few school accomplishments that made me proud.

What's the point of admitting to lying—an abject behavior that I teach my children is never acceptable? Simple. If it hadn't been for homework, I would have enjoyed school and learning and most certainly told fewer lies.

In his popular book, *The Homework Myth*, Alfie Kohn surgically destroys virtually every argument that traditional homework leads to improved learning or higher achievement. You'd be hard-pressed to find a single study suggesting that students at any level perform better academically because of homework, without connecting the study to overall grades or test scores—two barometers that tell more lies about learning than I did about missing homework assignments. Still, many educators continue to pile on the nightly worksheets and textbook chapters.

CHANGING THE NARRATIVE

Why is homework so pervasive in schools, in spite of overwhelming evidence that it does little more than make kids hate learning?

Longtime teachers, authors, and education consultants Starr Sackstein and Connie Hamilton answer this question and many others about homework in this groundbreaking book. But unlike the saber-rattlers who only rail against the practice, Sackstein and Hamilton change the narrative. You see, if brilliant researchers and orators, like Alfie Kohn, can't discourage teachers from assigning homework, it's doubtful that anyone can. Since homework isn't likely to disappear from students' backpacks anytime soon, educators and parents need more than admonishment. They need practical strategies for hacking homework in such a way that it will no longer be the monster that turns honest kids into liars. They need strategies that will inspire learning outside of school.

In *Hacking Homework*, the eighth book in the *Hack Learning Series*, Sackstein and Hamilton provide 10 strategies that teachers can implement tomorrow that will revolutionize how students and parents view academics outside of school. What makes this book so valuable is that it is truly for every education stakeholder—homework advocates, homework haters, skeptics, principals, parents, teachers, and even students. This is the book that will finally end the debate about homework and change how students work outside of class.

ABOUT HACK LEARNING

Education hackers are tinkerers and fixers. As with all hackers, they see solutions to problems that other people do not see. They are specialists who grapple with issues that need to be turned upside down or viewed with a different lens. The fixes they suggest may appear unusual at first, but as each chapter unfolds, their purposes will become clear and you'll be as eager as you've ever been to implement them immediately in your own classroom and school.

Inside

Each book in the series contains the revolutionary Hack Learning Formula—chapters, called Hacks, which are composed of these sections:

- **The Problem:** Something educators are currently wrestling with that doesn't appear to have a clear solution.

- **The Hack:** A brief description of the author's unique fix.

- **What You Can Do Tomorrow:** Ways you can take the basic hack and implement it right away in bare-bones form.

- **A Blueprint for Full Implementation:** A step-by-step system for building long-term capacity.

- **Overcoming Pushback:** A list of possible objections you might come up against in your attempt to implement this hack and how to overcome each one.

- **The Hack in Action:** A snapshot of an educator or group of educators who have used this hack in their work and how they did it.

I am proud to be the publisher of and a contributing author to the *Hack Learning Series*, which is changing how we view and solve problems in teaching and learning. When you finish reading this book, you will understand precisely how to rebrand and repurpose homework. You may begin to see solutions to other problems that you've previously overlooked. In the end, you might even become an education hacker.

And that's a good thing.

—*MARK BARNES, EDUCATOR/PUBLISHER/PARENT*

INTRODUCTION

It's time to reimagine homework

"DID YOU ALL do your homework? Put it in the homework basket and I'll grade it tonight. Yes, Kim, I see yours. Markus, I don't see yours. Make sure you get it to me tomorrow. Now let's get ready to learn for today."

What message does this lecture send to students about the value and relevance of the time they put into completing yesterday's assignment? The homework doesn't tie into what they're doing today, and there is no immediate feedback. Meanwhile, although Kim skipped her favorite TV show to do the worksheet while Markus played video games, their different choices have no impact on today's lesson. This is a lost opportunity for all involved.

If homework is assigned, it must be purposeful, transparent, and tied to learning experiences. Students shouldn't have to guess the reason for the homework, or worse, mindlessly complete assignments for the mere reason because they were told to do so. Secondary school teachers have close to 150 students; collecting work every day and providing any kind of meaningful assessment is almost impossible. It's not much different for elementary teachers with five core subjects to teach. After half an hour of grading, how many of us are guilty of flipping through the pile and just assigning a check or check minus depending on whether the work is complete? There isn't enough time in the day to comment on everything each child turns in.

Additionally, when teachers are expected to give homework assignments every night (whether because of district policy or parental wishes), there is no way they can all be constructive. It was this problem that spawned Hack 1: Break Up With Daily Homework, where we grant permission to teachers to sever the obligation to assign tasks at home simply because it's expected. In reality, there is a high likelihood that some assignments will be of poor quality because of the sheer quantity. So if we can't produce high-quality homework, what is the point of going through the motions? What message does this send to students about learning and their time?

As a parent, Starr believes nothing is more egregious than her elementary school child being sent home on a beautiful day in April with a backpack full of nonsense meant to prepare him for state tests. Once the sun finally comes out after a long winter, her son Logan is eager to run around outside, because young children need this—they don't get it enough in school, but we'll save that argument for another day. Instead, Logan must spend 40 minutes to an hour completing work that doesn't make him think, wasting valuable physical and social time with friends from the neighborhood who aren't in his class at school.

Since little research supports the claim that students in elementary school benefit from daily homework, why do we continue to burden both teachers and students with expectations that often ruin learning for our children? Students are doing too much already and they desperately need unstructured playtime to work out important social skills, which can't be learned on a worksheet.

These problems don't only apply to younger students. Connie's three teenage children have all had similarly exasperating experiences with homework. Her son Trey, for example, had teachers who assigned homework so that students could practice skills in preparation for the test. Trey is one of those kids who picks up classroom learning right away, isn't shy about asking questions, and can master content without the "practice" assigned by his teachers.

The explanation for the homework then switches to "He has to learn responsibility," which frustrates Connie and her son. Doesn't contributing to family chores, memorizing drink recipes for his job at the coffee shop, getting to ski practice on time, and helping his younger brother and sister with their homework count for building Trey's employability skills?

Connie's son Luke, on the other hand, is a non-traditional student, who hasn't embraced classroom learning yet. Homework was always a chore and a battle, but he did it. Now that Luke is in high school, he comes home with work he finds little value in and doesn't understand. Luke's interest in learning has dwindled over the years, leaving Connie with a few unsavory choices:

1. Argue and get him to figure it out on his own or to ask a friend for help.

2. Sit down with him and re-teach what he didn't learn in the classroom, giving his teacher the inaccurate impression that he had learned the lesson in class.

3. Put out a plea on the community Facebook page for a tutor and hope someone is available immediately and doesn't cost an arm and a leg.

4. Let it go and send him to school with a fistful of questions.

Parents with children who have struggled academically can relate to this experience and have likely been tempted to succumb to the idea that "It's not worth the fight." The teacher in Connie knows this isn't the best option and wants to push her son through, but the tired mom knows it's late and maybe it would be better to avoid the battle and let Luke go to bed instead of expecting him to teach himself what he clearly doesn't understand.

Finally, there's Connie's daughter Allie. She's a teacher's dream. Learning doesn't come easily, but she works hard. She's very aware of her weaknesses and has developed her own strategies for successful learning, such as listening to an auditory version of a book while reading. She does her homework diligently, without being prompted, and gives it her best effort.

The problem with Allie's approach to homework, however, is that she's working for the A. She focuses on things like neatness or the length of a paper, rather than creative reflection. She answers only the questions posed to her and rarely exceeds these parameters to explore the topic on her own. Occasionally, Allie will question the relevance of learning about a subject like Greek Mythology, but completes the homework anyway. What her teachers aren't tapping into is her natural curiosity for learning.

Allie has spent countless hours on YouTube learning how to apply makeup and organize her nail polish bottles. Meanwhile, viewers have watched dozens of videos that Allie has published about how to braid hair. In contrast, when Allie's homework assignment is completed, she views her learning on that topic as over. She's not inspired to inquire further and expand her knowledge, even though she clearly has the ability to initiate her own learning in other contexts.

Homework is one of the most misused tools in education. So many contradictory ideas are bundled inside the homework paradigm, with clashes between assigned learning outside of the school day, and play and learning in more natural ways. When we give students homework that doesn't directly relate to their lives, we are devaluing student time and disrespecting the sanctity of learning.

Every learner works at a different pace. After being in school for seven hours, shouldn't a child have the opportunity to reflect in a manner that is meaningful to him or her, allowing new learning to sink in before adding more practice? Shouldn't we spend less time assigning and grading homework for the sole purpose of marking a grade in the grade book and devote our energy to improving students' learning experiences?

We, of course, answer Yes to all of these questions, and this book is our way of encouraging you to reconsider the traditional view of homework and reimagine it in a way that makes more sense for teachers, parents, and learners. To accomplish this, the book is organized through a series of hacks—backward engineered from traditional pushback that is often given about why homework is essential. We tackle these challenges head-on and provide realistic solutions, through the What You Can Do Tomorrow, Blueprint, and Hack in Action sections of each chapter, offering practical answers and anecdotes of how these ideas are successfully implemented.

In Hack 6, for example, Justin Birckbichler highlights the importance of using student interests to incite curiosity and engage students beyond the school day by using content from his legal segregation unit to involve multigenerational discussion about the learning.

In Hack 8, Don Wettrick describes a student's research outside of school that inspired two full years of self-directed learning at home, which led to the student making a difference in her community.

Each chapter has contributions like these from experienced, progressive educators. The Hack in Action also provides annotations that we offer as a way of connecting these teacher anecdotes to the preceding strategies in each Hack. We hope our observations will spark your own ideas about trying something new with your community of learners.

EINSTEIN AND SHIFTING THE PERSPECTIVE

You will notice that Albert Einstein makes an appearance in every chapter with quotes like, *"Anyone who has never made a mistake has never tried anything new."* We were drawn to his thoughts about learning while writing *Hacking Homework,* so we begin each chapter with Einstein's words as inspiration to encourage the risk-taking we suggest. Traditional homework is an insidious practice that often ruins the learning process for children and puts a damper on playtime and learning as a positive experience. We believe learning outside of school should be as inspirational to kids as Einstein's words are to us.

Hacking Homework isn't written to solicit teachers, parents, and students to make picket signs with "NO MORE HOMEWORK" messages. We strive to shift the perspective on learning at home to be more exciting and relevant than what we experienced as students. Our belief is that learning shouldn't be a dreaded activity; learning can and does occur all of the time. The approach of teaching a new concept in class then assigning hours worth of drill-and-kill problems has proven to be unproductive, and we hope that this old-school method will change. We still want learning at home to continue but in a different way.

Bottom line: We want you to consider sound alternatives to traditional homework that foster a love of learning in all students and encourage them to learn outside of class, whether you tell them to or not.

HACK 1

BREAK UP WITH DAILY HOMEWORK

Work around the policies

"You have to learn the rules of the game and then
you have to play better than anyone else."
—ALBERT EINSTEIN

THE PROBLEM: SCHOOLS HAVE WRITTEN POLICIES THAT HANDCUFF TEACHERS FROM HACKING HOMEWORK

HOMEWORK IS OFTEN conceived of as paper-pencil tasks that are completed at home on a nightly basis; breaking from that tradition and perception can be a challenge. Some school districts actually require teachers to assign daily homework, based on the "that's the way we've always done it" rationale. When districts establish these types of policies, they take away teachers' autonomy to determine the most effective means of creating learning experiences both within and outside the classroom walls.

The
Dreaded
Ttwwadi
(That's The Way We've Always Done It.)

Amy @friEdTechnology www.friedtechnology.com

We send mixed messages to families when we promote family time, extracurricular activities, and student jobs, then infringe upon that time with nightly required homework. Keeping up with busy family calendars can be a juggling act, and sometimes reading for 20 minutes every night doesn't make the priority list. Not only can the nightly approach to homework be counterproductive, making students tired and hostile toward learning, it creates tension between parents and their children, leading some parents to resent the teacher or the administrators or both.

Curriculum materials often come with predetermined homework. Many teachers see it as mandatory, not optional. Also, creative assessments are often ignored when a textbook predetermines work assigned for home. Other issues with nightly homework include:

- Undermining teachers' ability to make choices for their students.

- De-emphasizing the value in clubs, sports, and other activities in which students engage after school hours.

- Expecting children to continue their "work" after long school days, which doesn't support what we know about child development.

- Predetermined homework makes assignments boring and irrelevant to students, lowering the level of effort they put in.

- Students view learning at home as an obligation, rather than an authentic opportunity to expand upon or spark more learning in the classroom.

THE HACK: BREAK UP WITH DAILY HOMEWORK

Schools across the nation are embracing the idea of eliminating at-home learning altogether, or at the very least, making it optional. If you're teaching in a system where change is slow and/or you're not given the autonomy to make decisions about homework policies, create a workaround. This way, you can honor some of the *Hacking Homework* philosophies without jeopardizing your career through an act of insubordination. In advocating for a shift in how your school approaches daily homework, begin to collect evidence on the successes you've had with tweaking your own practices.

WHAT YOU CAN DO TOMORROW

- **Stop giving homework every day.** Give yourself permission to deviate from the expectation of nightly schoolwork. Just because the math materials have a consumable workbook that parallels the unit, day by day, doesn't mean you have to use it. Students attend school for 30-35 hours a week. This schedule means heavy cognitive work for children. Some educators have voiced the perspective that school is the student's "job." We believe 30-35 hours a week is enough for a child and adding even an hour a night approaches what's considered overtime for adults.

- **Distinguish between "required homework" and recommendations to support learning.** Since there's a difference between establishing good learning habits and tasks that link to daily lessons, begin to explicitly make that distinction. For instance, share the benefits of reading at home with students and parents, but promote it as a way to read for pleasure, enhance vocabulary, build fluency, but not to fulfill a nightly homework requirement. Put yourself in the role of a pupil, then connect that to how you learn as an adult.

  When was the last time you read a book and thought, "I think I'll document the number of pages I read and the minutes it took me to read them. While I'm at it, I think I'll write a summary of the main idea of the text"? It doesn't make sense to require your students to break up the joy of reading with compliance tasks. If students are assigned 30 minutes of reading a night, some kids will set a clock, and no matter where they are in the text, shut the book when the 30 minutes are up. Lovers of reading choose to pick up their current book every chance they get and not because they are required to do it nightly. Other students will sit behind an open book and fake reading for 20 minutes and then slap a reading response into their log, during the last 10 minutes. So, the goal of encouraging students to read isn't fulfilled with an individual reading log. (Establishing a class reading log is outlined in Hack 1 of *Hacking Literacy* by Gerard Dawson.)

- **Define homework differently.** If you're stuck in a system that requires teachers to give nightly homework, then find a loophole. Hack the homework system by "requiring" students to: Go for a walk, share what they learned in class with a parent, play a board game, volunteer, or even call a family member from out of town, just to catch up.

A BLUEPRINT FOR FULL IMPLEMENTATION

Step 1: Discuss homework policies with staff.

Having a shared understanding of the role of learning at home is essential to developing an overarching school message and culture. Some schools use school improvement teams, while other schools have communications committees in which representatives from the school community come together to discuss important school policies. Starting the conversation and coming to agreement on homework's purpose opens the door to hacking. Questions for discussion include:

- What are the most recent research findings on the impact of homework?

- What data do we have regarding the impact of homework on learning (not grades...learning)?

- What message are we sending about family time when we require homework?

- If we must give assignments outside of class, what's a reasonable amount of time students should spend on it?

- How do students/families perceive homework?

- Is homework, as currently used, effective?

- Are there ways we can encourage learning opportunities without making them required "homework"?

Step 2: Provide evidence for the change.

When a district begins to abandon some traditional uses of homework, it's a shift that will require parents and students to adjust their preconceptions and expectations. While a number of them will likely support policies that discourage nightly homework, it's possible you'll run into others who are resistant to change. Being explicit about your intentions and rationale helps parents and students understand the reasons for deviating from the status quo. Examine Figure 1.2 for some examples.

Change in Homework Practice	Reason for Change	Additional Thoughts
Elimination of reading logs	We want students to read for pleasure, not for compliance. Students are encouraged to read at home a book of their choice and interest.	Consider having a family book club where everyone reads the same book and talks about it. Skype or FaceTime with Grandma, inviting her to read along with you.
Not everyone will have the same homework	Each student has unique learning needs. In order for academic practice to be helpful in learning, it should be not too easy and not too hard for students.	Although students might have different homework, the learning intentions for our classroom are consistent for everyone. This means even though students might be interacting with the content differently they're all still interacting with the same content.
Sometimes there won't be any homework	We recognize the value of family time and extra curriculars. We encourage students to be involved in activities outside of school and don't want homework to interfere with their ability take advantage of other opportunities	If your family has an off season or a student isn't involved in extracurriculars, take an opportunity to teach your child something you're interested in. Guitar, golf, or pick up a board game and power down once a week to help your child learn strategy and sportsmanship.

Figure 1.2

Step 3: Plan events that expand student experiences.

Learning isn't confined to the schoolhouse. Breaking up with the notion that students don't have to sit at the kitchen table completing assignments in order to learn does not mean that learning slows down. Instead, learning expands beyond the classroom, to a 24-7 timeline. Not every family, however, has the resources to enroll their children in piano lessons or sign them up for the soccer team. Consider ways that you can capitalize on less traditional learning environments to provide experiences to students and their families that support their social and emotional growth:

- Invite families to picnic on the playground

- Plan activity nights with music and an open gym (make it a family dance for younger students)

- Have tech nights so students teach adults how to use technology

- Coordinate a Battle of the Books

- Start a robotics or Lego team

- Plan a beautification club so students and/or families can make your school more aesthetically pleasing

- Partner with community centers so as to provide information on opportunities outside organizations offer

- Host Twitter chats to discuss various topics related to the interests of your community

- Connect students with e-pals to build writing and socialization skills

OVERCOMING PUSHBACK

There is a required number of homework grades each week. Data on student proficiency should take the form of substantive assessment, not graded homework. It's no secret for readers who follow us that we are proponents of standards-based learning and teachers throwing out grades. As this book is about hacking homework specifically, we'll simply point out that because we're unsure about the level of support a fourth-grader gets from parents, friends, or our pal Mr.

Google, any grade we give her for completed work might not accurately reflect what she has learned. So gather your assessment data from the classroom, not from homework.

If homework isn't assigned, kids won't do it. We are looking at the whole child. While state standards are certainly important for students' academic success, we're suggesting they only address one aspect of long-term success. Much of the time students spend outside of school on things other than academics have value too. If the "other things" aren't advantageous to kids' social and emotional growth, then go back to Step 2 and implement one of those ideas, or create your own. Kids are allowed to have lives outside of academic learning and they should. Let's support families the way they support us.

Parents expect homework. Don't underestimate parents' ability to support change once we have shared the rationale for reform with them. We can shift parents' perspectives by explaining the purpose and expectations of the new policy, arming them with clear strategies to support learning both when assignments are and are not provided. It could be helpful to communicate this information to parents multiple times, whether in writing, at an open school night, or during parent teacher conferences. Stay transparent and don't be afraid to field questions as they come.

Homework allows me to check student understanding. Sometimes we get the misperception that students are learning because they're compliant. They meet the minimum requirements for the grade or to avoid negative consequences, but not always for the purpose of learning. We see evidence of this when completed work is returned to school accurately, but students are unable to perform on summative assessments or even apply last night's focus to today's learning objective. This happens when students copy work, get highly scaffolded support from parents or peers, or simply rewrite what's in the text or their notes without really comprehending what's written. Inaccurate data results in unnoticed gaps in learning because students are able to hide their struggles behind shallow efforts on the work they are assigned to complete at home. Formative assessments in the classroom, where teachers can see and question students' application of the content, is a more accurate assessment of student learning than traditional homework that has little context and inappropriate support.

Students have to read every night to build fluency. The argument here isn't whether or not students should read at home. There have been countless studies that support reading at home. The bigger question is whether reading should be required as homework. We argue that students are more likely to develop a lasting love for reading if they read by choice and it's part of the family culture. Forcing students to read for a specified number of minutes—then document that they did so—undermines the goal of getting them to interact with literature in a way that is enjoyable. We're forcing a compliance task on an activity we claim is fun.

THE HACK IN ACTION

Bethany Hill is the lead learner at Central Elementary in Cabot, Arkansas, where she serves kids in pre-K through fourth grade. In this Hack, Bethany shares her experiences with getting rid of nightly homework at her school.

Bethany's Story

As a teacher, I always struggled with the idea of homework and often questioned its purpose. I assigned it every day because other teachers did, or because it was an expectation in the school. I remember thinking about how schools within the district had varied homework expectations, and how sometimes even classrooms within the school were quite different in what they expected from kids (and families). When I became the lead learner at Central Elementary, one of my goals was to establish consistency in homework policy, so that our kids and families could understand what we value the most.

The disparities in our expectations create confusion for students and families. Educators often have different ideas about what homework looks like and how kids should be held accountable for completing it, with the result that the tasks themselves become less meaningful. As we struggled to define the role of learning at home, this question surfaced: What can we do to help families understand the importance of engagement with their children? When we began to tackle this inquiry, our homework hack came to life.

AUTHOR COMMENT

Offering this kind of homework is one way to appease parents who are resistant to moving away from the traditional nightly approach.

At Central we chose to address the homework policy beast by setting an expectation for teachers, kids, and families to commit to family engagement. This includes reading, playing math games (many suggested by our school), family game nights, and free play outside.

Investment is the most important thing parents can give their children. For a kid, spending time enjoying his or her family's company is more beneficial to the home environment than being stuck at the kitchen table completing required assignments. We also shifted the focus of our school family night events from "training" or "talking at" families to different kinds of activities in which families can engage their children. Our goal in doing so was to provide a model for families, in the hope that these activities would be transferred to the home.

A small percentage of families questioned our intentions in not assigning homework, but individual conversations, our family night events, and feedback from their children eased their minds. Taking away the stress of having to study, read a certain amount, fill out a reading log, sign papers, or complete a math sheet has enabled us to focus on what really matters! We want our families to read to, with, and beside their kids. We want them to play games so they are supporting their child's social skills (winning, losing, taking turns). We want them to engage in unstructured play with their children at home, in order to foster creativity. We want families to go places together to help kids build their background knowledge about the world around them. How can we justify stifling these valuable activities in favor of mundane assignments? Family time is simply too precious.

AUTHOR COMMENT

In a survey or exit ticket, collect responses from parents about how they see learning happening at home. A week or so after a family night event, send a communication to families thanking them for attending and sharing the list of activities compiled from the survey/exit ticket with everyone — even those who were unable to attend.

Expanding the definition of nightly homework allows us to celebrate the learning that occurs in a diversity of formats. Shaking up our homework policy is one of the best decisions I have ever made for kids. True family engagement becomes possible when we weed out school policies that are unnecessary and that little research supports. Prioritizing the home and helping families support their children is our moral obligation. We can hinder family interactions with mandates and rules, or we can enhance them with guidance on what is truly important.

We often assume that kids don't like working at home, in general. When we asked students in our own schools and communities, there were a few anti-homework responses, but most students responded in a nuanced manner, recognizing the value of extending learning at home but suggesting a reduction in the quantity assigned by their teachers.

Here's what some students say about daily homework:

I feel while it's good at some days having homework every day isn't beneficial because it makes it feel like it's just an assignment made to keep the student busy. When the student feels this way then they start to care less of the homework and would leave it for the last minute. If the assignment was due the next week or students were given homework three times a week I think that would be better.
—BRENDON MUNIZ, HIGH SCHOOL STUDENT

If there is homework every night, I get a bit annoyed, especially if it is from the same class. I have band so homework is hard to fit into my schedule sometimes.
—FAITH GUERNSEY, HIGH SCHOOL STUDENT

I would dilute the gargantuan amount of it. I wouldn't eliminate it, but it's not fun when one has to miss events in their schedule or has to stay up an extra 3 hours just to complete it. We go to school almost 7 hours a day, nine

months a year, with class periods lasting over an hour. It is a good reference to see if the student is learning, but too much can be pernicious to the student's brain and life.
—JACKSON STEENWYK, MIDDLE SCHOOL STUDENT

I don't have one in particular but I can think of the days where I would be incredibly busy and doing homework would be the last thing I would want to do. I felt no motivation to put a lot of work into homework the days where I was balancing piano, sports, and theatre (all stuff outside of school). I felt like homework was taking up the time where I could be doing something fun.
—RACHEL BARNETT, MIDDLE SCHOOL STUDENT

It usually takes me longer to do my homework than other kids. Sometimes, I have to choose between homework and spending time with my family. I hate it when my dad invites me to go for a run to get ready for my cross country meet and I can't practice because I'm still doing homework. It's like I have to choose between two things that are both good for me, but homework always wins. It's not fair.
—ALLIE HAMILTON, MIDDLE SCHOOL STUDENT

Homework would be OK if we didn't have so much of it.
—STELLA, ELEMENTARY SCHOOL STUDENT

If I had homework, I would need a later bedtime so I would have all that time to do it.
—HUNTER, ELEMENTARY SCHOOL STUDENT

HACK 2

TEACH ORGANIZATION AND RESPONSIBILITY IN CLASS

Ramp up accountability, and time management skills

"Try not to become a man of success, but rather try to become a man of value."
—ALBERT EINSTEIN

THE PROBLEM: TEACHERS USE HOMEWORK TO TEACH RESPONSIBILITY

TEACHERS OFTEN CLAIM they use homework to teach responsibility, while rarely providing strategies to help students in this area. Of course we want students to be able to manage their time, meet deadlines, do quality work, and take ownership of their learning, but simply doling out assignments doesn't achieve these goals. Giving homework in the hope that it will magically build responsibility is unreasonable. This approach also clouds the purpose of learning experiences, making many stakeholders wonder if at-home learning is intended to assess responsibility or student learning.

Teaching is a challenging profession. Of course it would be nice to have classes filled with young minds capable of managing their time and diligently completing their work, but we respond to their lack of accountability skills by blaming their struggles on them with declarations like, "Guess you should have done your homework; maybe this will teach you to be responsible." That's like saying to a diabetic who goes into a coma because he doesn't know how to manage his condition, "You should have taken your insulin shot; maybe this will teach you to be responsible." If we have a student who needs to monitor her blood sugar, we teach her what to do. The same philosophy applies to students who are disorganized or lack responsibility. Let's look beyond the symptoms and tackle the root of the problem by keeping the following in mind:

- Just because students are told to do homework, this doesn't mean they have the organizational skills to complete the task.

- If students display a lack of responsibility, teachers often address this problem with *more* homework assignments, academic support, and punitive reactions, instead of direct instruction on accountability and time management.

- Employers want workers who are responsible, but the curriculum rarely includes lessons that specifically teach students how to develop these skills.

THE HACK: TEACH ORGANIZATION AND RESPONSIBILITY IN CLASS

We can agree that students of all ages lose papers, waste time, and have their priorities out of whack. Kids are often branded as irresponsible simply because they lack organizational and accountability skills. In order to effectively tackle poor habits, we should provide direct instruction and models of best behavior, teaching students how to keep track of deadlines and class materials; how to manage time efficiently; and how to be accountable for their work. Arming students with these strategies allows teachers to shift their focus from simply assessing whether students are responsible and organized to actually building responsibility and organizational skills.

WHAT YOU CAN DO TOMORROW

There isn't a one-size-fits-all solution to getting kids organized and developing their sense of responsibility. Each student might need a little something different to help him/her move toward becoming an independent learner. Teachers are working harder than ever before; much of this time is spent tracking down missing assignments, and planning consequences and rewards for completing all of their assignments. We're not often surprised to see the same names of students who lack the organization and responsibility skills over and over again. Our efforts to encourage accountability don't often change behavior.

In these cases when our best efforts don't produce results, it's more likely that those students just don't know how to keep track of assignments or manage time because nobody has ever taught them those life skills. We don't have to turn our curriculum upside down, but let's look for opportunities to introduce and strengthen organizational and accountability skills, expanding beyond the traditional approach of assigning homework.

- **Maximize planners to manage time.** For elementary students, planners are often used as a diary of the day's events. Students copy a sentence or two off the board as a way to communicate from school to home what happened today or a reminder for what to bring tomorrow. Instead of using a planner to exclusively document each day's events, model how a detailed calendar helps them to plan. When you send home a monthly calendar, ask students to enter the events into their planners, getting help from parents if needed. Encourage them to add family activities as well; this will create a complete picture of what a student needs to plan around for his/her time. In class, regularly prompt students to look forward in their planners to consider what they have coming up in their schedules. Perhaps a favorite aunt has a birthday next week—the student might choose to use this event as the theme for a poem about the aunt as a gift. Teaching students to plan ahead will reduce procrastination and highlight the benefits of thinking about how to manage time instead of watching it fly by unproductively.

- **Make calendars age-appropriate.** For older students, teachers often provide copies of the syllabus with important dates up front, giving students the opportunity to plan out long-term learning goals. Take this to the next level by introducing students to reminder messages within Google Calendar. As they enter due dates, students can determine how much notice they need in advance. Some students might send themselves a "get started" reminder message while others would benefit from "project is due in 3 days." This personalized approach to teaching them how to manage time honors individual students' work habits in a way they won't feel nagged but still have beneficial reminders.

- **Target effective learning characteristics.** With your students, brainstorm qualities that support learning. As students identify traits, document their responses. Their lists might include qualities like: smart, enjoys reading, keeps track of stuff, follows directions. Take this list and divide qualities into categories: knowledge, responsibility, attitude, etc.

  Then, depending on the age of your students, create common definitions of these category labels. Good and bad examples of what different traits look like will further clarify definitions. This list could be displayed in the classroom as a reference throughout the school year. Some teachers even have their classes sign the list, as evidence that students will strive to personify these traits. If you have multiple classes, each group of students should create their own unique list of words.

- **Demonstrate responsibility through classroom jobs.** Having a job chart in the classroom not only helps you

41

carry out your duties, but also provides students with a sense of purpose and daily responsibility that is visible in the classroom. The tasks should be of such a nature that students are held accountable for doing them, and that failure to do so would be conspicuous. For example, if a student is responsible for gathering attendance data at the beginning of class, it's an important task that would certainly be noticed if missed. If a student has a prearranged absence, another layer of accountability would be for him or her to solicit a replacement. This type of setup in the classroom makes the many layers of responsibility visible to all students. When someone is absent, the rest of the class sees the impact of how important it is for the role to be filled and the affect it has on everyone if it's not. See Figure 2.1 for more examples of classroom jobs that provide students the opportunity to show responsibility.

- **Illustrate accountability with think-alouds** that naturally arise in the classroom.

  This might sound like:

  I'm not going to be in class tomorrow. What responsibilities do I have that will not be taken care of if I'm not here? My class job this week is communicator, so I need to talk to the student substitute to have her fill in for me tomorrow. I'm also going to need to find out what I missed. I will alert the secretary to let him know I'll be touching base with him when I return to class the following day. Actually, if I text him after school tomorrow, maybe I can get the information tomorrow, finish it tomorrow night and then I will be ready to learn and not behind when I get back the next day.

- **Acknowledge responsible acts.** Give recognition to students who implement the classroom norms you have established. Contact the parents of those students and provide explicit examples of how their children displayed responsible behavior in the classroom. Take an extra minute to ask the parents what they do to instill a sense of responsibility at home. If the parents put forward some good ideas, feel free to apply them in the classroom. If the parents express a need for support in this area, take the opportunity to partner with them by offering them examples of how responsibility and time management could be developed at home.

JOB BOARD

Inventory Managers: Responsible for making sure everyone in their group (could be table, or row of desks) has all the necessary tools or supplies to complete a task.

Edison: Responsible for powering up any technology the class will be using or checking devices in/out of the storage cart.

Disseminator: Responsible for distributing papers to students.

Taskmaster: Responsible for keeping a schedule, monitoring the time to make sure the class stays on schedule, and if necessary, making modifications to the schedule.

Scribe: Responsible for creating a summary of class lessons and providing notes to absent students.

Chief Spokesman: Responsible for crafting communications such as notes to parents, blogs, and tweets.

Understudy: Responsible for replacing a student who is absent and not able to fulfill his/her job duties

Figure 2.1

A BLUEPRINT FOR FULL IMPLEMENTATION

Step 1: Collaborate with fellow teachers on norms for learning.

In collaborative teams, share the lists of norms you and your students created, as described in the "What You Can Do Tomorrow" section. Look for common themes and identify key skills that you want students to hone. Together, create an agreed-upon list of traits through which mini lessons on responsibility and other desirable skills can be developed. Teachers should provide opportunities for students to practice these traits during the school day and at home. This approach gives a purpose to work done at home and develops students' ability to meet learning standards. Telling a student to do homework and punishing him/her when that doesn't happen fails to foster responsibility. Without instruction on how to balance time between track practice, dinner, and youth group, it's not likely youngsters will just figure it out.

Step 2: Generate examples of learning traits.

In order for students to arrive at a shared understanding of the desired traits, it is important to provide evidence of what responsibility looks like and how responsibility impacts their learning and the classroom culture. Asking students to give non-examples or antonyms can get silly, but is also useful. Students are more likely to remember your common definitions when you present both types of illustrations. You can use a Frayer Model (see Figure 2.2) to further clarify vocabulary words that might be unfamiliar to students. Use questions like these to visualize learning traits:

- What does organized look like vs. disorganized?

- What are the effects of being disorganized?

- How can we move toward being organized consistently?

This step of guiding students to identify the transferable skill deepens their understanding of the words defined in the "What You Can Do Tomorrow" section.

Frayer Model Diagram

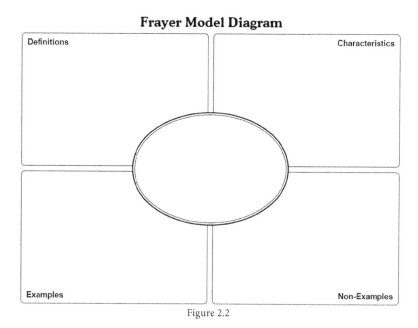

Figure 2.2

Step 3: Embed lessons that teach responsibility skills.

If you find yourself saying, "I shouldn't have to teach my students to _____; they should know how to do it by now," that's a good indicator that you do have to teach or re-teach expected behaviors. Using the list of responsibility traits created in Step 1 and the definitions you and your students clarified in Step 2, now construct lessons addressing each of the traits, including organizational skills and responsibility. Even after the lessons are over, continuously refer back to the traits to highlight how these habits are vital to both school and life.

Step 4: Implement chances for responsibility skills demonstrations.

When we assess responsibility by checking whether homework has been completed or not, we're missing the true definition of the word "responsibility." Is the student who copied off his friend, cut and pasted from a blog, or had his/her parent do most of the work just as responsible as the student who approaches the teacher during class to explain extenuating circumstances that prevent timely completion of an assignment? We don't know a teacher out there who wouldn't embrace a student's initiative in explaining that she has a soccer game tonight and won't be home until late. Almost all of us would work with the student to reach an agreeable plan to work through this type of time constraint. This is a teachable moment, not only for the individual student with the conflict, but the entire class.

We suggest using a fishbowl protocol in which students and teachers model these types of "responsibility" conversations for the class. In a fishbowl, a discussion or dialogue is held in the center of the classroom while participants circle around and listen to/watch the conversation. Role-play of the soccer game scenario not only highlights the benefits of being proactive, but also facilitates the transformation of students into hackers themselves, ready to devise solutions to their problems instead of excuses. It might sound something like this:

> **Sophie:** I know our science reflection is due tomorrow, but I have a soccer game tonight so can I just turn it in Monday?
>
> **Teacher:** Thanks for coming to me ahead of time to let me know you're having a problem with the timeline. Let's look at some creative ways you might be able honor the deadline and win that game tonight. What options have you considered?
>
> **Sophie:** Options? I didn't think of any.

Teacher: Well, how much time do you need to finish the assignment?

Sophie: About 15 or 20 minutes.

Teacher: Think about your schedule tonight and see if there are 15-20 minutes between the end of school and bedtime when you can get it done.

Sophie: I could do it on the way to the soccer game.

Teacher: That's an option. Any other times?

Sophie: Maybe after I get home, but if we win we will stop for ice cream.

Teacher: Let's plan on a win and assume you'll be getting ice cream. Any other times?

Sophie: Maybe I could ask my grandma to pick me up from school a little later today, and I could quickly do the homework before I go home.

Teacher: That seems like a good option. Any others?

(Continue this exchange to help Sophie identify every possible option)

Teacher: So you've identified time on the bus, immediately after school, right before bed, or early tomorrow morning before school. Of those choices, which one will work best for you?

Sophie: I think I'll call my grandma and get it done after school. That way I can focus on my game.

Teacher: Sounds like a plan. Nice work solving this problem and making sure you keep your responsibility of meeting the due date.

After the fishbowl, students observing the exchange between Sophie and the teacher discuss the benefits of this conversation. Perhaps more important, students can evaluate what would have happened if Sophie had not communicated her dilemma to the teacher and had arrived at school the next day without having completed her homework.

The fishbowl protocol is beneficial for both older and younger students. Many elementary teachers use this strategy to engender citizenship on the playground or kindness in the classroom. Consider the systems you already have in place and integrate opportunities for students to model their organizational skills, accountability, and responsibility.

Step 5: Transfer strategies to support students at home.

What parent doesn't want his/her child to grow up to be a successful adult with good character? Working with parents on these types of skills will not only strengthen your relationship with them, but will also lay the groundwork to create connections between student behavior at home and student behavior at school.

> When rewards and punishments don't impact certain students, we often ramp up the consequences, but the results don't change.

When you communicate with parents, be explicit about how you plan to teach students to be responsible. Let them know how your students have defined traits in Step 2 and suggest ways that parents can support implementation of these traits at home. In this chapter's Hack in Action, we share an educator's process for teaching students how to organize papers. This same system can be used to help students clean out their closets. Look for opportunities to reinforce desired traits at home. If you really want tasks done at home to teach kids how to get organized, then perhaps an effective way to achieve this goal is to encourage young students to help mom and dad organize the toy box, or older students to organize the refrigerator so food doesn't spoil.

Step 6: Revisit the classroom norms for learning all year.

The habits referenced in this Hack must be revisited and rehearsed often; we can't simply check them off the list and believe our students will magically become organized and responsible independent learners. Development of these traits must be an ongoing process, and teachers should always be looking for ways to reinforce the skills. Keep a time-slot in your classroom for revisiting the list of traits and adding strategies that you, students, and parents have found to be successful. You don't need to reinvent the wheel. Opportunities for organization and accountability are everywhere: We just need to be more intentional in taking advantage of them.

OVERCOMING PUSHBACK

Incorporating behavioral skills into academic instruction is a significant adjustment for some teachers. In a desperate effort to encourage students to complete homework, teachers often use external incentives, such as grades, stickers, and praise; or they go with punitive actions, like lunch detention, a negative note home, and a grade drop. When these rewards and punishments don't impact certain students, we often ramp up the consequences, but the results don't change. Instead, if the root cause of students not continuing their learning at home is behavioral, we should provide direct instruction on responsibility and organization. Intentionally pinpointing these positive behaviors will effect real change in the students' approach toward their education.

It's my job to teach, it's the student's job to learn. Teaching is just talking if learning doesn't occur. It can definitely be challenging to help young, developing minds see the long-term value in education. However, there's a reason education is compulsory. Students are not given the unilateral power to determine whether they want to learn. If they appear unwilling, uninterested, or unmotivated, it is our job as teachers to find ways to inspire them and give them the skills to complete their tasks. Students who are apathetic toward school are unlikely to wake up one day and suddenly see the value of extending their learning outside the classroom. If lack of organization and responsibility are barriers, let's break it down by teaching these skills directly, not by hoping students will pick them up through homework.

I don't have time to teach employability skills. You don't have time *not* to. If you could add up all the time you spent giving students another copy of missing work, lecturing them for incomplete assignments, and grading work that might have been copied from a peer, you'd have time to write a book addressing employability skills. Just like we take the time to teach procedures at the beginning of the year, to ensure a smooth flow for classroom learning, the time spent teaching students what it means to be responsible and how to implement organizational strategies is invaluable.

My secondary students will see a job chart as babyish. Relate it to having a real job. At the beginning of the year, post a "help wanted" bulletin board with job descriptions and applications. Offer how these roles can be included in letters of recommendations for college applications as evidence of accountability. Stress how colleges want students who are dependable and are willing to take on responsibility for their learning and support the learning of others. You could even host mock interviews and "hire" for the posted positions.

THE HACK IN ACTION

Tamra Dollar has taught at both the elementary and secondary levels and most recently, as a middle school literacy coach and creative writing teacher. She believes all students can learn, just not on the same day, in the same way, and at the same pace. She shares Confessions of a Literacy Coach on her blog, Dollar Literacy. In this Hack in Action, Tamra describes how she turned excuses into learning opportunities to help students grow more responsible.

Tamra's Story

Over the years, I've heard more excuses for missing work than I care to admit. Long gone are the shallow excuses like "The dog ate my homework." As you can imagine, preadolescents are savvy and seem to know the perfect excuse to use and exactly the right moment to deliver it.

Without question the coup de grace of all excuses is the one that shifts responsibility from the student to the teacher. The excuse goes something like this: The student looks the teacher squarely in the eyes and solemnly swears that he/she has already turned in the homework. It is the teacher's fault for losing it.

In a stroke of genius, the problem is transferred from the student to the teacher. If you're like me, some days it is not worth going to extremes to convince the student that the homework is, indeed, missing.

Three weeks later, the homework surfaces during a mandatory locker clean up. It is now stuck to another piece of paper with a sticky substance that smells like cherry.

In order to tackle this kind of scenario, a colleague of mine started a lunch club to help students get organized. The club would order pizza and kids would have a grand old time playing trashcan basketball with old papers, only to find out a week later that a slam dunk had been a critical worksheet. Students had placed papers that were clean back into their notebooks, removing all those that looked untidy, but had no other check/balance system for determining whether something was worth keeping. The club disbanded after a year.

AUTHOR
COMMENT

Tamra's co-worker successfully discerned that the issue with homework wasn't ability and perhaps not even motivation. The students just weren't able to keep track of all the papers and deadlines. They didn't have a system for staying on top of it all. Tamra's school was on the right track in allocating time for students to get organized. If students do not have instructions and a workable process, however, they are not likely to figure it out on their own.

As part of my reading intervention class, I decided to dedicate the first Monday of every month to teaching organization. (If I had a new student I would schedule a time to meet with him/her one-on-one). I would have my students bring in their backpacks and every scrap of paper they could find in their lockers, even if the scraps looked like trash.

At a table or on the floor, I would have the students write on three sticky notes: Keep; Trash; or a "?". The first pile was for papers that should be kept and organized, including incomplete assignments, study notes, schedules, etc. The second pile was for papers that should be trashed or tossed out; students would often find doodle sheets, drafts of papers that had already been rewritten, and even multiple copies of the same paper. The third pile was for papers that the student did not know whether to keep or toss. Students were taught how to assess the purpose of the paper so as to determine if it should go in the keep or trash pile.

I would literally pick up each piece of paper and ask, "Is this to keep, trash, or you're not sure?" When students caught on to the system, I sat back and cheered them on. Next, the student would sort the "keep" pile by subject, then place papers in the appropriate subject folder. I added an extra layer of support by keeping piles two and three in the back of a filing cabinet until the end of the semester. Many times important papers "look" like trash! It was inevitable that a student would run into my room in a near frenzy because he/she threw away a paper that was due.

Students thereby learned through experience how being organized can save the day. They began to create their own systems for the "?" pile, just in case they might need papers from it next week. Students who are learning how to organize often do not have the

AUTHOR COMMENT

As students are applying their newly learned skills, giving them a safety net is an additional strategy that teachers can temporarily use.

skills to prioritize what is or isn't important. My reading intervention classes gave them a baseline framework within which to do so.

Teachers use this type of best practice in regard to academic content, like how to multiply fractions or write an expository essay. Explicitly teaching students how to organize is a way to teach responsibility.

If students don't keep track of their assignments and commitments, then they can't manage their time, leading others to view them as irresponsible. As educators, we recognize that just like the

Pythagorean theorem must be taught before it is mastered, organization is a precursor to the ability to hold oneself accountable and act responsibly. This Hack is one example of how to provide direct instruction on skills that will enable students to be successful in life, not just school.

We recommend that teachers develop lessons and/or classroom routines that develop these vital life skills, creating regular opportunities for practice. Daily homework assignments, as discussed throughout this Hack, are not the answer. However, when teachers assign the type of out-of-class work discussed throughout the book, organization and responsibility will play major roles in students' success. So, they will develop valuable life skills and apply them to learning outside of school. That's a win-win.

HACK 3

CULTIVATE RAPPORT

Establish positive relationships to motivate learning

"It is the supreme art of the teacher to awaken joy in creative expression and knowledge."
—ALBERT EINSTEIN

THE PROBLEM: DAMAGED RAPPORT INCREASES POWER STRUGGLES

THERE ARE NUMEROUS reasons that students don't do work at home. As discussed earlier, sometimes it's because their schedules are just too busy. When students feel like their teachers don't like them, their drive to perform well declines, creating an additional obstacle for teachers to overcome. Students attach the negative thoughts they have about their teacher to the learning process. "I don't know why my teacher is making me do this…"

When students dislike teachers, this only exacerbates any animosity students may already have toward class work they have to complete at home; these feelings then spill over into learning in general. When learning is viewed as "work," and students are expected to do it to avoid negative consequences, the message about learning becomes twisted. Power struggles over homework ensue, sending the message that schools prioritize completion of the task over embracing the opportunity to learn and celebrating the growth that comes along with learning. These foundational beliefs drive this Hack:

- Teachers who connect with students are more likely to get quality work from them. Authentic conversations about progress and growth occur when there is a trusting relationship.

- The culture of the classroom sets the stage for student attitudes toward learning both in and out of the classroom. If the teacher uses scare tactics, such as "You'll get a lunch detention if you don't do it," students grow averse to learning experiences and are less likely to follow through with activities at home.

- Conversations that concentrate on learning and the progression of learning keep the focus on mastery, rather than completion. Power struggles blur the purpose of learning at home, distracting from the ultimate objective of mastery.

THE HACK: CULTIVATE RAPPORT

If we are invested in moving every child where he or she needs to be to achieve mastery, relationships are the most effective way to obtain this goal. So why should homework be any different? It's easy enough to say that students just won't do it, but if we invest our time in knowing who our kids are and what they need, we can easily reduce the power struggles that hinder effective learning extensions at home. As we re-imagine what learning outside the classroom is, we must include them in the conversation. Otherwise, we will spend our time fighting with them to turn in work that they've often copied just to get it done.

Building trust and rapport with students gives us a window into who they are as individuals, deepens our understanding of their pre-ferred learning styles, increases their motivation, and prevents the power struggles that damage the culture of our classrooms. This Hack, as well as others in the *Hack Learning Series*, addresses what we can do to develop relationships with even the most challenging kids.

WHAT YOU CAN DO TOMORROW

- **Greet students with a smile.** You've heard the phrase "Actions speak louder than words." When you make welcoming students a priority, you not only send a message to the entire class that they are important to you, but you are able to read students' faces and postures to see if there's anything off about them today. A quick check-in to let them know you care goes a long way. Even this subtle strategy to build trust will benefit your students when it comes time to engage in learning outside the school day.

- **Notice the small things and say something.** Students love it when people notice things about them, even the kids who go to great lengths to blend in. Are those new shoes? Did you get a haircut? How was the birthday cake last night? These interactions convey to students that you're interested in them as individuals and not just focused on the lesson.

- **Play "get to know you" games.** Learn about your students through icebreaker activities. Instead of just playing the name game at the beginning of the year or semester, play two truths and a lie, where students write two little-known facts about themselves and one that is untrue. You and the other students try to figure out which one is the tale. You can play this game over and over again, mixing it up by creating new categories for truths and tales, such as food, free time, and hair. These little-known facts about students will come in handy when you're providing examples of transferable skills and explaining how the knowledge students acquire in class applies outside the school walls.

- **Use growth mindset language.** Stop praising students for their intelligence. Compliments like "You're a genius" suggest that students either have the ability or don't. These comments do not promote hard work or a desire to become intentionally thoughtful about learning. As students see themselves as capable learners, they will be more confident in their pursuit to take the lead of their own growth. Refer to Figure 3.1 for ways to reframe your feedback.

Instead of:	Try saying:
You're a brainiac.	Your hard work really shows in... (be specific)
You have a knack for writing.	I can see you've been working on your voice. What a great improvement in your writing.
I'm so proud of your good grades.	You must be so proud of yourself, all that effort really paid off.
That was easy for you because you're so smart.	Looks like that wasn't a good match for your skills today, I'll make sure you're challenged tomorrow.
Try harder next time.	What can you learn from this so you can continue to improve?

Figure 3.1

A BLUEPRINT FOR FULL IMPLEMENTATION

Step 1: Make your data visible.

During the "get to know you" games discussed in "What You Can Do Tomorrow," keep track of details students share. Once you've collected information about students, share it. If 75% of your students are really into science fiction, you're providing justification for the reason you've elected to have them read a text on time travel. Then, displaying data you've collected showcases how much you care about each child while promoting an atmosphere of trust and rapport. Knowing their passions will arm you with the opportunity to make suggestions for texts, current events, articles, and/or trivia for students to explore outside the classroom.

This approach is beneficial beyond content interests. Be aware of skills and talents students have. If you know students are uploading tutorial videos to YouTube for fun, prompt them to use that skill to film how to find and calculate angles found around the house or invite them to create a video of famous quotes from Abraham

Lincoln and synthesize what it says about him. When this positive culture exists in your classroom, power struggles are naturally reduced and students are willing, actually motivated, to jump into the learning and extend it when they get home.

Step 2: Establish a plan of action with at-risk students.

When students have difficulty in class, they're likely to have struggles out of class as well, so you'll want to get to them quickly. Set up a time to meet with learners to initiate a conversation about what the barriers are to learning. When you are able to identify why students are not complying with learning tasks, you know how to address the problem. Never assume that you know why students aren't completing activities.

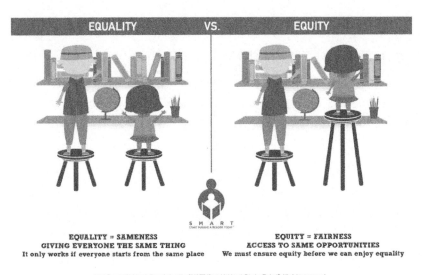

EQUALITY = SAMENESS
GIVING EVERYONE THE SAME THING
It only works if everyone starts from the same place

EQUITY = FAIRNESS
ACCESS TO SAME OPPORTUNITIES
We must ensure equity before we can enjoy equality

Figure 3.2

If students don't understand the lessons, they might need intervention. But if they have to babysit other siblings because they have a single parent who works a second shift, intervention is not the best solution. Sometimes, teachers think that they have to provide the same level of support to every student. If one student gets extra attention, it may be viewed as unfair, and that support is revoked. When you look at learning as a progression toward mastery, however, you must make sure students get what they need when they need it. Student needs are too diverse to support a cookie cutter approach. Figure 3.2 provides a visual of equality vs. equity. Remember that not every learner needs the same supports to gain access to learning. Fair doesn't mean equal.

Students will appreciate the individualized scaffolds and you'll see greater success across more kids. If it doesn't happen naturally, softly shift the conversation about how students can set themselves up for success when learning at home. If it helps for them to read in a quiet spot in the classroom, how can they provide that same type of atmosphere at home? Maybe she waits until her younger sister goes to bed, or he wears headphones when reading is involved at home. It's the defining of the problems that make for the best solutions, so take your time to clarify the obstacles to learning together with the student, then identify solutions that will work in all learning environments.

Step 3: Converse with all students about their progress regularly.

Sometimes any additional moments in the school day are spent establishing a plan as outlined in Step 2. There is a missed opportunity if we don't find some time to guarantee that all students have reflection time on their academic progress. Build a schedule that allows you to spend a little extra time with as many students as you can over the course of a day. Snag a moment with the early arriver who is always there before class begins. When students are working independently, tack a minute or two onto the end of a one-on-one conversation, expanding the dialogue beyond the current class activity to the student's overall thoughts on learning. Consider this exchange between a teacher and student and notice how the teacher hones in on one strategy that can spread in other areas:

Teacher: I noticed when you were working in class today that you were singing or talking to yourself, and even doing a little dance? Tell me about that.

Student: I was having trouble remembering all the Great Lakes. I know we learned H.O.M.E.S. to give us the first letter of each lake and I can remember that, but I still couldn't remember the actual lake names…especially Lake Superior.

Teacher: How did you help yourself remember Lake Superior?

Student: I wrote down the list of lakes, and my dad helped me make up a way to sing each lake. Then we added some motions to go along with it. Superior is like Superman, so I do this (student puts one fist in the air as if she's going to fly). I don't know why it works, but it does. I can remember all the lakes now and that helps me as we learn about Michigan history.

Teacher: That's called a mnemonic. It's a very useful strategy to help remember things. Remember in math we used "Hey diddle diddle, the median's the middle, you add then divide for the mean. The mode is the one you see the most. The range is the difference between"? That's another example of a mnemonic. Have you used any others?

Student: OHH! Yes! Order of operations, Please Excuse My Dear Aunt Sally.

Teacher: That's right. But in social studies you created your own mnemonic. How did that help you?

Student: I added a way to sing it to myself, it was much easier to remember. Maybe I can use that for writing to help me remember to transition my paragraphs. I'm going to think of one tonight.

Teacher: What a fantastic strategy. Would you be willing to share your mnemonics with the rest of the class tomorrow, especially the new one you write tonight about transitions?

Student: Really you want me to teach the class? Yea. It's going to be so good everyone will want to use it.

Even if students don't appear to be experiencing problems, establishing a rapport with them could be key to effective support if something changes in the future. In these student conferences, ask them for their thoughts on the pacing and rigor of the class, as well as their perceptions of their learning progress. Sometimes students are capable of creating their own hacks to obstacles, and because they've gotten used to doing so, appear to have it all together and fall off your radar. During these metacognitive exchanges, students are reflecting on their learning strategies that they take and use wherever they go, not just in school. These are the nuggets that foster lifelong learners and provide students with the confidence to persevere through challenging concepts when they want to extend learning at home.

You never know what these few minutes with a student will uncover. Knowing a student wakes up at 4 a.m. every day to catch the bus from the babysitter's house might be helpful information to have if he begins to fall asleep in class, or doesn't always have his materials with him. This enlightenment that might be revealed during a chat with a child is likely to influence your perspective on what and how much work is sent home. These realizations of what your students' lives are like at home confirm the need to reconsider traditional homework.

Broaden the discussion to show you care about the student: Inquire about how a student's clan castle is coming along, or how many stuffed animals the collection is up to. In this type of natural dialogue, the topic might be shifted to books students are reading at home or passion projects they have initiated. If a student is rebuilding a motorbike, explicitly ask him how he can use what he learned in the garage in today's science lesson. As mentioned, these quick conversations can happen spontaneously: before the bell, while you're waiting for students to line up in the hall between classes, or wherever you find a moment to connect. It's not necessary to carve out half of your instructional time to shoot the breeze with kids. Purposeful links between learning at home and school is an effective way to guide these chats.

Step 4: Be an active listener.

When students display their trust in you by disclosing information that doesn't reflect favorably on your lesson, resist the urge to be defensive. Just pause, listen, paraphrase, and take note. Ask them to identify ways you can help, or if they have any input into what would increase interest. When the conversation focuses more specifically on doing assignments at home, pose questions to encourage students to share the challenges they face. You might discover that a student doesn't have a computer and has to complete assignments on his phone. Another student might disclose that her single mom just started taking classes and while she's studying, your student is responsible for getting her younger siblings fed and off to bed on time. During these valuable moments, you're able to get a glimpse of the true barriers to learning.

Conversely, when a student tells you she spends most of her evening FaceTiming with her friends, it would be natural to pass judgment about how she is prioritizing her time. Instead, take advantage of the rapport you're developing and find out what they're discussing. Are they fans of a favorite TV show? Do they collect anything with butterflies on it and share their collections? Have they learned to do origami by watching videos together? What you learn might come in handy when making connections to future in-class lessons and ways these students can naturally extend their learning at home. Imagine suggesting they determine if symmetry is used in butterfly wings or if it's relevant in folding paper. Interacting with students at this level might be one of the best ways to send them running home to apply their new learning.

Step 5: Rinse and repeat.

Throughout the school year, repeat Steps 1-5 in order to continue building trust and mutual respect with each of your students. These relationships will result in students taking your advice and will supply you with the information necessary to develop a plan of action in support of their individual needs. The goal is to create independent learners so as you revisit these steps, students will build the skills necessary for them to take charge of their learning and extend it out-side of school. Giving them the strategies to build on their strengths and compensate for their areas of weaknesses is the greatest gift we can offer for their ongoing success in life.

OVERCOMING PUSHBACK

Establishing a foundation of trust and rapport is invaluable. Think of co-workers you've had that you respected versus others who cre-ated power struggles. Which collaboration style provided an atmo-sphere for you to flourish? Students will eagerly partner with teachers who show an interest in them as learners and as individuals. When a teacher's main focus is on compliance, and learning is secondary, the priorities are out of order. Students might do what they're told, but no more. If we want them to take more initiative in their growth, we should leverage on our positive relationships and build a climate for open conversation about how learning occurs in school, but also continues after the 3 o'clock bell. When you come up against push-back, consider the following responses:

They might not like their bosses, but they will have to do the work. True, but you're not their boss; you're their teacher and the role of a teacher isn't the same as that of a supervisor. Additionally, think about past bosses you've had. Were you more or less likely to go above and beyond for a boss who appreciated you and cared about you as a person, or someone who was ready with a write-up for you to sign before even asking why you were late?

I'm their teacher, not their buddy. Also true, but if you build rapport with students, it will not only benefit them, it will make your day-to-day job less stressful. Reducing power struggles with individual students creates relationships that value and promote learning everywhere, including at home.

Some students are really hard to like. True again, but they're kids. We can't label them as unlikeable at age 10 just because they're pushing back on completing traditional homework or don't seem to like you.

THE HACK IN ACTION

It's natural, when a school sees achievement gaps, to first look at curriculum and instruction for potential change. It's not uncommon for staff to assume that more time on studies will increase student achievement. Since there are only so many hours in the school day, some schools increase the amount of homework they issue to students, thinking it will help. In this Hack in Action, Connie discusses how the school improvement team included students in the problem-solving process and learned how teachers' rapport with students impacted students' attitudes about learning and homework.

Connie's Story

Connie's school district was informed by the State of Michigan that one of their schools, Saranac Junior-Senior High, was a Focus School. Focus Schools are identified as having the largest achievement gaps between their highest and lowest achieving students. In order to be removed from the list of Focus Schools, a school would have to—within three years—improve the achievement levels of the bottom 30% of their students (B30s) and close the achievement gap.

Staff identified students' lack of motivation in regard to homework as a key problem, dedicating meeting after meeting to brainstorming ways to induce B30s to complete their assignments. We simply couldn't figure out why they didn't care about learning and couldn't see the connection between doing their homework and success. One teacher suggested we meet with B30s and ask them directly. So we did. A group of teachers and hand-selected students met for a roundtable discussion with coffee and donuts. Over the course of two hours, we asked the B30s all the questions we had been pondering for years.

- How do you feel about school?

- What causes you to pass some classes and not others?

- How could the school improve to help you be successful?

- And the biggie: Why do you do your homework more often in certain classes?

In response to this last question, we expected to hear things like "if I have time... some classes are too hard... I don't like reading..." and so on. However, we were slapped in the face with a consistent message from the entire group of low-achieving students. They overwhelmingly agreed that they were willing to do homework and put forth effort in classes if they felt that the teacher cared about their learning and underscored how they would use this content later in life.

One young man, representative of our unsuccessful learners, told a story about how his English teacher, Mrs. Cindy Sanford, cared more about him and his learning than he did. He acknowledged the time and effort she put into feedback, and said, "I didn't think it was right that she spent more time on my homework than I did." Mrs. Sanford was not at the roundtable to hear his comments. She is a highly respected veteran teacher known for her caring demeanor. It was no surprise that the students recognized Mrs. Sanford's compassion, but we couldn't ignore the negative feedback also provided by the ladies and gentlemen sitting with us: Students viewed as the "tough guys" of the school.

One of our female students mentioned that although she was great in one subject, she couldn't stand the teacher who taught it, bringing to mind the adage: "Students need to know how much you care before they care how much you know." It was the perspective of these students that the teacher no longer loved the job and couldn't wait for retirement in June. We severely underestimated the impact relationships, positive and negative, played on students' feelings toward learning both in and out of school, so we became more intentional about building rapport with students. This systematically helped us better connect with kids and improved achievement at our school.

Instead of placing "carrots and sticks" in front of students to bribe or scorn them for doing or not doing their homework, we took the time to identify root causes of their attitudes around it. According to students, connecting with them to help them see the value in education, writing, and even proper grammar—and then figuring out what works best for each individual student—makes a difference. After the conversation with the B30s, the school improvement team at our school shared the students' perspectives with the entire staff, launching conversations about how to improve rapport with students.

It's not always an expensive speaker or a new curriculum that helps students see the value in learning, including learning at home. After two years, Saranac Junior-Senior High closed its achievement gap and saw its name removed from the Focus List. While a variety of initiatives contributed to this progress, the two hours the staff spent listening to students' perspectives was crucial.

Building better relationships with students allows teachers to really get to the heart of student motivation. The more invested we are in students, the more compelled they are to take initiative in our shared spaces; continuing learning outside the classroom is just one part of this philosophy. We have to stop wasting time fighting with kids who won't do homework and spend more time getting to know them and trying to figure out why this is the case.

Forcing compliance through punitive measures and extrinsic rewards will not make struggling kids smarter or more capable. In such instances, we must examine what we're asking kids to do and then determine if these tasks will successfully cultivate a love of learning in each child. It's okay to be flexible and meet kids where they are. Choose battles wisely and then everyone wins.

HACK 4

CUSTOMIZE TO MEET STUDENT NEEDS

Be flexible with assignments and timelines

*"It's not that I'm so smart, it's just that
I stay with problems longer."*
—ALBERT EINSTEIN

THE PROBLEM: HOMEWORK ISN'T ONE-SIZE-FITS-ALL

HAVE YOU EVER sat in a professional development (PD) session and wondered why you were there, because nothing new was being presented, or the speaker's message didn't relate to improving your teaching? The one-size-fits-all approach to learning isn't productive for teachers and it's less effective for kids. If we know that students are all at different spots in terms of learning progression, why do we dish out the same assignment to every student? The following notes were considered when developing this Hack:

- We spend the entire day catering to the individual needs of students, using flexible grouping and individual conferencing, then wrap it all up by telling every student to do the same task, regardless of how much or little they understand.

- Assigning tasks that are too easy for students reinforces the belief that it is pointless busy work and creates resentment on the part of students and even parents.

- Because students learn at different paces, some students might attempt to complete assignments at home with an underdeveloped understanding of the material. Ensuing mistakes become embedded in students' minds, making re-teaching the content difficult.

THE HACK: CUSTOMIZE TO MEET STUDENT NEEDS

Students make significant progress when teachers scaffold lessons in order to push learners slightly beyond their levels of comprehension. If the gap in understanding is too wide, students are frustrated and are quick to give up. If the gap is too narrow, students get bored and learning ceases. On top of academics, student interest and individual backgrounds also come into play with the relevance of learning. Understanding the broader purpose and the transferable life skill helps students see how their work connects to short-term learning goals and long-term outcomes.

When assignments exist in the sweet spot of learning, efficacy and engagement spike. Think of crafting activities done outside of school, like a video game designer. If kids experience enough success but are challenged, they will stick with the game, even begging for one more chance to get it right. However, if they rapidly make it to the highest level and win the game, the fun is over and they're not interested in playing again. Once is enough.

On the flip side, if a game is too hard and kids get stuck on a level for too long, they'll cheat or quit. See any connections to homework here? We're not saying out-of-class assignments have to be a video game. What we are suggesting is that customizing activities to meet the needs of your learners is key to facilitating student growth and engagement.

With this kind of transparency, students make the necessary connections and are more inclined to prepare outside of school for upcoming in-class lessons and activities.

WHAT YOU CAN DO TOMORROW

- **Delay sending work home that students cannot do independently.** Much of the frustration around traditional homework stems from students not remembering what they did in class that day and therefore feeling like they can't complete the assignment. Delaying out-of-class assignments that require application of a new skill—until there is a high level of certainty that students have sufficient foundation to execute the task—makes students' time more productive.

- **Prompt exit tickets that identify ways they can extend learning.** When closing a lesson, give students a sticky note and tell them to put their name on the back or the sticky side of the note. On the front, ask students to name two ways they could extend their thinking on today's learning. This will not only give you information about if they grasped the learning target for today, but also get them thinking about how to go deeper. Next, sort, or allow students to sort them into categories such as research, transfer to home, create an example, etc. These extension opportunities for students to implement at home came straight from students, and offer choices for them to deepen their learning by choosing their own ideas or using someone else's.

- **Construct out-of-school activities at the independent level**: According to Lev Vygotsky, The Zone of Proximal Development (ZPD) is the point in students' learning progression at which they have enough background knowledge to be able to learn, but still require support and guidance. This is where the magic happens. When we assign work for students to do at home in their ZPD and provide no assistance, we can expect frustration, leading to struggles with parents and tears of anger at the study table.

  Many curriculum materials follow a sequence that introduces a new concept and provides application opportunities immediately after the lesson. It's not uncommon for teachers to start these tasks in class, then ask students to finish them at home. The problem is that teachers often don't check to see if the content is in the ZPD. Teachers need to clarify the material and draw connections to the next lesson in the sequence if they want students to be confident. This moves assignments out of the ZPD, where scaffolds and supports are needed, and at an independent level to foster success at home.

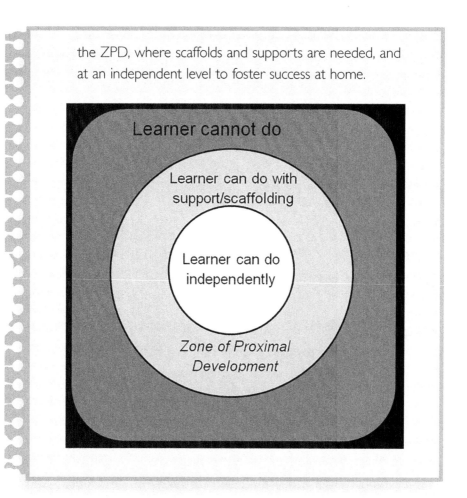

A BLUEPRINT FOR FULL IMPLEMENTATION

Step 1: Review your unit plans.

As you're planning your lessons and aligning them to your scope and sequence, pick out some of the main focuses of each day and summarize them in a few words. Consider what can be done in class and if there are any pieces that make sense for students to tackle at home. Looking at these focuses as a progression will help you determine how best to customize work for students.

Step 2: Present timelines of upcoming learning experiences.

This timeline doesn't have to be detailed. A good way to communicate your plan for the class is through a link to a Google Calendar on your class webpage.

Sample lesson sequence:

Monday: KWL on volcanoes

Tuesday: Read article on volcanoes, update KWL, add another source

Wednesday: Gallery walk sharing other sources, update KWL

Thursday: Check for understanding, watch video, update KWL

Friday: Show what you know assessment

Step 3: Identify short- and long-term assignments.

In the sample lesson sequence in Step 2, you might be planning for students to bring in their own sources of information about volcanoes on Wednesday. It would make sense at the introduction of the lesson, or even the Friday before, to invite students to begin looking for videos, blogs, webpages, books, articles, etc., on volcanoes and be ready to share on Wednesday. If you flag this piece of the unit in advance, you can launch your lesson in the KWL on Monday and include anything the students learned through collecting the sources you'll use on Wednesday.

This is a low-pressure, but useful assignment to give to students. It will only take a few minutes, gets them thinking about volcanoes in advance, and doesn't require prior knowledge or application at home that will create power struggles between students and their parents. If the students come in on Monday and don't have their sources yet, you'll be able to highlight the advantages gained by the students who completed that task over the weekend, and can also revisit the week's agenda, reminding students that without outside research, Wednesday's activity will not be as productive as it could be. With this kind of transparency, students make the necessary connections and are more inclined to prepare outside of school for upcoming in-class lessons and activities.

Step 4: Communicate learning intentions.

Some districts use learning targets, others call them learning objectives or learning goals. Regardless of what you call the intent of your lesson, there must be a clearly defined purpose. When teachers are clear—not only about the task and how to complete it, but about why the task helps them learn, what they are expected to learn from it and how they will know they have learned it—students focus more on the learning intention and less on completing the task. This approach affirms that the point of working at home is to learn, not just to complete an assignment. This approach reinforces the notion that each person can take different paths at different speeds to achieve the same learning objectives.

Ineffective example	Effective example
Homework: Watch a YouTube video and write a paragraph on your opinion about the video.	Learning intention: Link opinion and reasons using words, phrases, and clauses Criteria for success: Write a paragraph that includes words that link opinions and reasons. Homework: Using a YouTube video as your subject, provide evidence that you can link opinion and reason.
Sample response: This video on silly cats was funny. I laughed when the cat got pulled into the bathtub. I was surprised to see there were cats that weren't afraid of water. I think you should watch this video too.	Sample response: I've always thought pets were funny, specifically cats. Some people think that cats are afraid of water but actually some cats enjoy baths. There are many YouTube videos that provide examples of how funny cats can be. I think you should watch them too.

Figure 4.2

Step 5: Personalize learning.

Conducting a learning style preference survey is a valuable tool when assigning customized work. Intentionally selecting approaches that match a student's preferred method of learning doesn't dumb down the learning, but personalizes it for students. If the objective is clear and students understand the criteria for success, the means through which they might fulfill these criteria varies. Ask yourself:

- Could the student have used a piece of text to write an opinion using words that link opinions and reason?

- How about a teacher prompt asking the student about his/her favorite flavor of ice cream?

- Does that task need to be paper-pencil?

- Could the student record his/her paragraph in an audio message and send it to the teacher?

Maintaining a focus on learning but being flexible about the "how" will make students far more likely to follow through on the plans they have developed.

Step 6: Adjust based on student progress throughout the unit.

If students have extended time to complete tasks, checking in with them periodically prevents them from procrastinating and becoming overwhelmed by the amount of work that has piled on over time. Adjusting as needed doesn't always mean giving students more time. If a project or assignment is completed in less time than provided, this is a perfect opportunity to talk to students about making conscious decisions regarding how they will use that additional time. Is it best to get a jumpstart on another project? Are they interested in learning more? Could the additional time allow them to pursue a different passion? These opportunities allow students to think proactively and creatively about how best to plan out their schedules. Invite students to contribute to the conversation about customizing their learning and the pace in which they learn.

Step 7: Offer regular feedback about progress.

When you've provided clarity on what students need to know and how they will be able to show they know it, your discussions with them should remain focused on the criteria for success and the means through which students are working toward the learning objectives. In Figure 4.2, the learning intention and criteria for success center on linking opinions and reasons. The student should have focused on providing that evidence, and in the second example, the student did. You might be tempted to send these students back to the drawing board to work on expanding their vocabulary. However, if the expectations were clear from the beginning, students wouldn't feel that the time they spent was wasted.

This can be further clarified by making sure the student understands success criteria upfront, and encouraging a dialogue through questions along the way. Regularly checking in with students throughout the formative process and providing specific feedback that aligns with moving their learning toward the success criteria.

OVERCOMING PUSHBACK

Fighting against what has always been done will be a challenge. Rethinking what we ask students to complete outside the school day may cause a little stir. Here are some issues you may face when customizing it:

I write my lessons day by day based on what my students need. This blueprint isn't asking for step-by-step lesson details; it's a rough outline of where you anticipate you will be going. If you are a teacher who creates lessons the night before, then take the opportunity at the end of the day or class period to reflect out loud on how you're using observations from the day to mold the specifics of subsequent lessons. You don't have to completely change your planning style, just give students a glimpse of how they can plan ahead and make sure that the learning occurring in and out of the classroom takes the personalized processes into consideration. Each day we should be assessing for learning, taking what has happened and adjusting accordingly the same way we expect the students to.

I have too many students to personalize learning for all of them. Whenever possible, involve students in identifying ways they can best achieve learning objectives. Staying focused on the learning intention creates freedom as to how to accomplish learning targets. Offer a few explicit options and invite students to add to the list. There will be more detail on this strategy in Hack 8.

What if students don't do homework at all? If your purpose for giving activities at home is similar to that of Cathy Cooper's in the Hack in Action, then it's not an issue if students don't complete their work at home. Her intention as an elementary school teacher is to create a connection between home and school, so the tasks are optional. If you're assigning out-of-class work as a requirement and students don't complete it, determine the reason and address the cause, not the effect.

This sounds like a grading nightmare. The work you gather from different students should provide information about their progress toward a learning objective; the manner in which students complete the assignment is less important. If you're worried about a different grade for a student who creates an infographic vs. a student who sings a jingle, you might be focusing on the wrong thing. Instead, you should be asking the questions, "Were the students able to show what they know, and how close are they to meeting the learning targets?" Remember, assessments are assigned to standards and learning goals, not individual assignments. If students have shown some evidence of success when working independently at home on a concept or skill, you're ready to assess their ability to transfer that more formally in a summative way.

THE HACK IN ACTION

Cathy Cooper is a teacher at Saranac Elementary School, the PK-6 building in the district where Connie is curriculum director. Mrs. Cooper has taught many elementary grades, and in this Hack in Action, describes a system she uses to customize homework.

Cathy's Story

As a teacher of various grade levels within an elementary school, I have learned to remain flexible in all areas of my role. Homework is no exception. I have adapted homework to meet my needs and the needs of students and parents, as well as to ensure a "developmental fit" based on the ages of my students.

Because we are aware that homework in the elementary grades has a negligible impact on learning, I tend

AUTHOR COMMENT

As Mrs. Cooper reiterates the lack of research supporting homework at the elementary level, keep in mind that while there is some support for assigning homework at the secondary level, the benefits of it do not increase the longer students spend on it. Fifteen minutes of homework has the same effect on learning as three hours.

to look at it much differently from the teachers I had when I was a student. My primary purpose in providing activities for students to complete at home is to create a connection between school and home: honoring family time but providing parents with a view of what students are learning in class. Because out-of-class activities are not tied to a specific day's lesson and aren't designed so that the learning of material occurs at home, I intentionally select activities that reinforce skills and allow students to show off their knowledge to parents, but in a brief show-and-tell approach rather than drill and kill.

Our standards identify spelling as one area in which students need to show proficiency. Each student in my class has his/her own spelling list based on words they are using in their writing. I recommend spelling as a place to start because it allows parents to establish routines, it's an easy skill to apply, and can be practiced in many ways. I offer suggestions such as using sidewalk chalk to write words on the driveway, smearing shaving cream in the bathtub, and singing the spelling words to the tune of a favorite song in the car. These types of at-home activities allow families to engage in their typical activities and throw in a little learning on the side, which does help customize the learning to each family.

An unintended benefit of highlighting alternatives to "write the word 10 times" is that parents are able to break from their preconceived notions of what homework and learning traditionally look like, which helps them engage in this more personalized and meaningful approach.

In order to allow families to create their own routines around school connections and study time at home, it was critical that I choose a consistent day of the week to send home their customized tasks, asking that they be returned no later than the same day the following week. I use Friday because in my school we send home

Friday communication folders. Parents and students know to look for the homework on Friday. I then request to receive it on any day from Monday through Friday of the following week. I do not offer reminders or "nag"; I simply expect that the packet will be returned before a new one goes home again the following Friday, allowing students to determine the best timeline for that week together.

Some students hand in partially completed work, which I accept. Occasionally a student will not hand in anything one week, but the following week I may find two assignments in the folder. Students know that I do not "grade" the homework, but look at each assignment and respond to what has been completed. When I review their work, I am checking for some understanding of the material, and offering feedback. I often make comments about how I can tell their efforts at home are having an impact on their learning, encouraging them to choose to support their own learning because they see the direct effect. Any data I gather is used for small group and individualized instruction.

The activities designed for home are based on a child's interest level and academic need. For example, if I were to include a personal interview activity about sightseeing in Michigan and I have a nonverbal student or a student who recently moved from out of state and has little to no connection to the area, I would craft different assignments that are more meaningful and relevant for these students.

AUTHOR COMMENT

Giving students a full week to bring their work back to school honors family time and provides an opportunity for students to apply time management skills.

As educators we all have students working at a variety of levels and I might have four to six different math activities or games going home with individual students on the same Friday. I want my students to spend time connecting school to home at appropriate levels for themselves. If, during a formative assessment, I notice a student needing a "little extra," I make a note to include that "little extra" for the child the next Friday. But that certainly doesn't mean I expect all of my students to complete the extra activity. In order to effectively customize homework, I must know my students well. I enjoy the process of creating something somewhat unique for each of them.

Most students will consider traditional homework a waste of time when it isn't relevant, is redundant, or is beyond what students can do independently and appropriate scaffolding isn't available. Tell us you've never heard of a student copying a friend's assignment: not really learning the material, but still completing the assignment. Then there are tasks we think will take 10 minutes but wind up invading valuable family and extracurricular time because they are too difficult for students. Those 10 minutes turn into an hour.

While no teacher would ever deem these examples ideal, we can't discount how common they are. Teachers can prevent these negative outcomes by more intentionally considering the learning preferences/levels of each student and customizing homework to address his or her respective learning needs.

HACK 5

ENCOURAGE STUDENTS TO PLAY

Support innovation and creativity

"Play is the highest form of research."
—ALBERT EINSTEIN

THE PROBLEM: BORING HOMEWORK
TAKES AWAY FROM PLAYTIME

TOO OFTEN TRADITIONAL homework is laborious and boring. Some teachers don't worry much about engagement or the manner in which students complete the work; they focus only on what students must learn in order to prepare for the upcoming exam. Because of the expectations imposed by content-heavy learning, teachers employ a top-down approach, paying little attention to student needs. Students are forced to complete worksheets and meaningless assignments that discourage curiosity and creativity, preventing students from taking ownership of their learning processes and robbing them of unstructured playtime.

Here are the main concerns with the absence of play due to uninspired nightly tasks:

- Teachers often have a lot of content to cover and not enough time in class, so they feel the need to transfer material left over from the school day into after hours. The homework is focused on student absorption and memorization, not student interest.

- Boring homework doesn't encourage or support students' critical thinking, which is really what school is all about.

- Play, though extremely valuable for a student's learning progression, isn't considered "real work" that can substitute for content that needs to be covered. Instead, play is thought of as something that should be done on a kid's own time, once schoolwork is completed.

THE HACK: ENCOURAGE STUDENTS TO PLAY

With all the stresses that students currently face, it is essential that we, as educators and parents, encourage our children to make time for play. Play can encompass a range of activities; not just games or outdoor sports, but all structured and unstructured activities that students choose to do on their own time, such as reading, music, or painting.

There are many benefits to children engaging in play that help facilitate reflection on the day's events. With games like hide and seek or board games like Sorry!, for example, students are negotiating with each other and learning the same critical thinking skills necessary for school lessons. The more we offer students opportunities to do the things they love outside of school, while connecting those activities to what was learned, the more they will approach learning from a fresh and engaged perspective during the school day.

It is vital that all teachers spend time encouraging students to find their passions and then incorporate these passions into classes. Such connections are what make school more tangible and meaningful, helping students learn classroom material in the long term, not just for the day of the exam. For more innovative ideas on bringing play into learning, check out Angela Stockman's *Make Writing Hack 3: Teach Them to Tinker: Play through the process,* moving away from worksheets that don't really engage students in any kind of meaningful way.

WHAT YOU CAN DO TOMORROW

- **Throw out worksheets**. This is so easy to do. Start by integrating technology. In lieu of the worksheet with 20 problems, send students on a quest for problems of their own. Have them search the Internet or engage peers on a social network. If you're uncomfortable with technology, invite students to create the practice that you might send on a worksheet. The conversation alone will engage students and improve learning, and this is how kids play.

- **Re-evaluate the amount of homework assigned.** Assess what you're expecting kids to do at home and how long it will likely take them. Ask yourself if all the assignments are necessary and then try to lessen the load wherever you can. Students will then have more time to play after school.

- **Designate time specifically for play.** Instead of asking students to do worksheets, build playtime into at-home learning time, connecting play to students' education. Students learn so much from both unstructured and structured play. Ask them to play a board game that involves math—like Monopoly or Yahtzee—with family members. Students will benefit from the math practice, as well as the skills associated with this kind of play: patience, following directions, analyzing, sharing, etc. You can also bring board games into the classroom and use them to explicitly teach certain skills. For older students, consider a game like chess or Risk that gets them thinking strategically.

- **Connect playtime to learning.** Sometimes what we think is obvious isn't. So take time in tomorrow's class to connect all of the amazing skills that come out of play to the learning happening in the classroom. For example, ask students to tinker with writing, an art project, or a science lab for one period and then ask them to reflect on what skills were being used. Start a chalk talk in which students write on chart paper about what learning occurred as a result of their tinkering. In sharing their observations, students will realize the ways in which we are constantly learning in various environments. Remind them that this kind of learning begins outside of the classroom, often in ways they wouldn't normally consider, like while playing games.

- **Survey students about after-school activities and play.** Find out what students are doing on their own time so that you are able to make specific connections to their interests and activities in future classes/ units. Surveys can be issued using Google Forms, SurveyMonkey, or the well-worn pen-and-paper method.

A BLUEPRINT FOR FULL IMPLEMENTATION

Step 1: Pinpoint learning situations and communicate skills.

Before students can connect their play to learning standards, you must take the time to teach them how to discern and communicate about learning situations. In class, spend time working on communication skills like writing notes and making good eye contact, then connect speaking and listening standards to real-world skills. One way to reinforce this connection is by asking students to create and perform skits that emulate home situations. This would work well in preparing for student-led conferences using the work done in class.

As a scaffold for the process, help students write a script, if necessary, to figure out how to talk about what they have learned in a structured and meaningful way. This step can be implemented not just with older students but with students of all ages. Imagine kindergarteners telling their parents about why a square is always a rectangle but a rectangle isn't always a square. What a fantastic way to inspire learning outside the classroom.

Step 2: Share class work with parents.

Many schools already have communication systems that teachers use to share work that is going on in their classes. Find the system that works best for your age group of students and make sure to invite parents. Most applications also have the capacity for mobile notifications, if parents think this would be helpful. It's easy enough to set up shared spaces through platforms such as Google Classroom, FreshGrade, Edmodo, ClassDojo, Remind, Appletree, IO Education, etc.

The simple fact is you just never know where and when awesomeness will show up.

In order for parents to best facilitate connections between play and learning, they must be aware of what is happening in class. In addition to posting sample assignments or exemplary student work on shared spaces such as websites and social media pages, teachers can livestream lessons via Periscope (be sure to have signed waivers), giving parents a window into the actual classroom. This way, you take the sharing of class work one step further than just sending home a folder with worksheets. School will be a living, breathing experience that parents can partake in by either watching videos or live footage.

The more parents are engaged throughout the day, the better they can advance student learning at home, linking playtime to the classroom. Of course, this is yet another way to get families on your team, as we will highlight in Chapter 9.

Step 3: Connect learning standards with play.

As an extension of what you already started per the "Connecting playtime to learning" section explained in *What You Can Do Tomorrow,* it's time to connect the standards to the play. This will take time because there are many standards that can be taught through different forms of play. Spending class time drawing connections with students will establish a direct link between something fun and learning, helping them see where they overlap.

Speaking and listening standards, for example, easily align with play activities: "Adapt speech to a variety of contexts and communicative tasks, demonstrating command of formal English when indicated or appropriate" can be applied to every play situation. When we play with different friends and/or people of different ages, the way we speak to them hinges on what we know about them.

Being able to read an audience and appropriately communicate our feelings, thoughts, and ideas is part of what the Common Core aims to teach students of all ages. There are also specific math and content-area standards that align with games requiring strategy and/or money manipulation. Teachers shouldn't underestimate these connections. Check out Hack 6: Prioritize in Mike Fisher's *Hacking the Common Core* to learn about making the standards work for you. This is a helpful resource, even if you don't use the Common Core.

Step 4: Develop a list of out-of-school activities based on play.

In class, prompt students to brainstorm a list of potential home activities or games that relate to learning and their interests, and then describe how the activities will help develop their skills. A carousel brainstorm protocol would work well to accomplish this:

- On chart paper, identify environments students often frequent outside school, such as their neighborhoods, their homes, playgrounds, the local coffee shop, auntie's house, etc.

- Assign students to work in small groups at first, to ensure that all voices are heard, and have them list as many activities as they can think of that could take place in these environments.

- Next, have students list how the activities contribute to their learning.

- After small groups have documented their ideas for potential at-home activities, do a full class share of the proposals.

For a more kinesthetic version of this brainstorming process, have students write home activity ideas on small pieces of paper, write class activities or skills on other pieces of paper, then create piles connecting the two. In drawing these links, use colors to differentiate skills, constructing a colorful wall space in the classroom that will serve as a point of reference. For example, red might be associated with listening skills/standards, blue with speaking, green with organization, etc. Continue adding to the wall space throughout the year.

Step 5: Connect learning, social, emotional, and physical growth (Step 4 of this blueprint) and "play."

Students must be responsible for the out-of-class work they have chosen from the menu they created. With younger students and English learners, try using sentence stems like: "At home, I _____ which helped me learn to _____." This framework will give students a way to articulate what they did and how it connects to the learning happening in school. For older students, the link between play and education will likely come up in classroom discussions and small-group learning. Hold students accountable by asking them to make these connections explicit in their written reflections, when submitting work as a part of their process writing. This will be a more authentic learning experience than traditional nightly homework.

OVERCOMING PUSHBACK

Play is an essential part of childhood, but there will always be people who favor traditional homework for its strict nature. Parents and other educators may push back against the idea of students having more playtime with any of the following:

Play can happen at any time and shouldn't factor into homework. Although play can occur at any time, it doesn't happen enough, or with sufficient purpose. Because school has gotten much more serious even for younger students, play is essential to helping connect learning to life in a meaningful and enjoyable way. These connections are what will make lifelong learners out of our kids. As people get older, they begin to call play activities hobbies; these hobbies serve a key role in adults' personal lives and help them balance career and home.

School is more important than social time. Yes, school is important, but it isn't more important than social time. Consider the whole child when you're putting together educational plans. Social-emotional skills are a huge part of what teachers seek to develop in students. There often isn't enough school time to spend on the social-emotional, so these skills must be fostered at home with the help of family, friends, and educators.

What about kids with multiple parent homes? It's true that students of divorced or separated households face challenges, such as when families don't communicate with each other. We can include all households in the student's learning process by getting contact information from both parents for the purposes of Steps 2 and 5. There is no reason for the non-custodial parent to be less involved. As a divorced parent,

Starr shares custody of her son and has worked with Logan's teachers to ensure that multiple copies of important materials are sent home or mailed to both houses. Teachers also communicate regularly with both Starr and her ex-husband about Logan's progress. Such communication is vital to drawing connections between play and learning, as parents may not understand this philosophy at first. In order to truly advance learning through play, play must be a part of learning in both households; then there will be the necessary continuity to make learning stick.

There isn't sufficient time in class to finish everything. There are many things that you must get done during a school day, so re-evaluate the pace, scope, and amount of content you expect students to take in on a regular basis. The fact of the matter is that although you may be able to cram more into the day, that doesn't mean students are absorbing it all. Wouldn't it make more sense to slow down, focus, allow students to digest the learning in a meaningful way, and *then* move on when appropriate for all children involved? It may be tempting to argue that tests require a certain amount of knowledge, but let's teach for kids, not tests. Remember, stuffing all of the content into the day neither produces better test results nor fosters a lifelong love of learning. Instead, when we allow students to mix up learning with activities associated with play, we let new learning sink in and help kids actually enjoy the learning process.

THE HACK IN ACTION

The simple fact is you just never know where and when awesomeness will show up. Every teacher knows what we're talking about. Still, in traditional school situations, teachers tend to over-plan, leaving little room for students to explore and discover on their own. However, the more we put kids in situations in which they make their own decisions and generate their own ideas, the richer the classroom culture becomes.

Peter Cameron is a teacher with 20 years of experience at the junior level. He is an Apple Distinguished Educator, SMART Exemplary Educator, Google Educator, and an experienced leader in integrating all types of technology into the classroom. This highly experienced educator favors 90 minutes of daily homework. Yes, you read right, and we approve. Check out Peter's unique homework, which he has repurposed and rebranded as HomeSHARE.

As a student I despised the word homework. Images of sitting at the kitchen table for hours on end, beating my head against a textbook as I tried to complete an endless number of meaningless math questions or memorize 20 words for my spelling dictation, are forever imprinted in my memory. However, with my parents' support and patience, I persevered to complete the work. When I became a teacher 20 years ago, I did what every other good teacher had done before me: I assigned homework. I would task students with finishing an often-large quantity of math questions; completing a reading response journal and grammar sheet; and studying for our weekly spelling dictation and a number of other unit tests.

My views on homework have changed over the course of my career. I've arrived at the conclusion that traditional homework has done little to improve my students' academic performances or their ability to think and learn. In fact, I believe homework has had somewhat of the opposite effect. When it piles up, stress increases and students come to school tired, overwhelmed and burned out. I have also found that students who have little support from their parents or guardians (whether in regard to assistance with their assignments and/or encouragement to finish it) tend to turn in incomplete work, increasing the gap in learning for this group of kids.

Homework in my classroom has now evolved into home'share'. A couple times a week, my students are tasked with sharing a piece of writing with a parent, solving or explaining the solution to a "real math" problem, or creating a problem of their own that can be solved through play. I encourage parents to write comments on their child's work and initial it after their child has shared it with them. The result? Students are consistently completing home'work' in my classroom. Parents say they feel more involved in their child's learning and that the stress level within households has decreased.

| Week of: _____ Home"work" Name:_____ |
| Do one or more of the following for a minimum of 90 minutes everyday! |

Monday	Tuesday	Wednesday
Play outside____ Exercise____ Create something____ Meditate____ Talk with parents____ Read a book____ Volunteer____	Play outside____ Exercise____ Create something____ Meditate____ Talk with parents____ Read a book____ Volunteer____	Play outside____ Exercise____ Create something____ Meditate____ Talk with parents____ Read a book____ Volunteer____
Thursday	**Friday**	**Saturday**
Play outside____ Exercise____ Create something____ Meditate____ Talk with parents____ Read a book____ Volunteer____	Play outside____ Exercise____ Create something____ Meditate____ Talk with parents____ Read a book____ Volunteer____	Play outside____ Exercise____ Create something____ Meditate____ Talk with parents____ Read a book____ Volunteer____
Sunday	**Reflection**	
Play outside____ Exercise____ Create something____ Meditate____ Talk with parents____ Read a book____ Volunteer____		

I have also started to experiment with a new type of daily home'work' that encourages students to live more active, balanced lifestyles. For the last two weeks of the 2015/16 school year, I gave this assignment to my students: "Homework: Do one or more of the following EVERY DAY for a minimum of 90 minutes: play outside, exercise, create something, meditate, talk with parents, read a book, volunteer." I sent a note home to inform my students' parents and provided a tracking sheet.

The Monday after this new home'work' was introduced, my students arrived in class excited about how easy their assignment had been to complete and eager to discuss the things they had created, the books they had started to read or continued to read, and the types of exercises they had done. We had a conversation about "volunteering" and what that may look like (offering to help a neighbor, parent, or sibling were all deemed good examples of volunteering). A student inquired about how he might meditate at home (we use the 'Calm Classroom Initiative' at school) and his peers offered a number of suggestions. We also discussed the importance of balance and challenging ourselves to try things that we haven't done before.

AUTHOR COMMENT

Like Peter, many students despise traditional homework. This is the problem we are trying to address. Admittedly, getting rid of homework altogether may be impossible, but as suggested here, a home'share' allows us to create fun out of the 'work' assigned after the school day ends. Home'shares' also connect families to the learning happening throughout the school day even if the child isn't with them all the time.

My students continued to complete their homework with much enthusiasm during the last two weeks of the school year. After the first week, 92% of my students handed in their completed tracking sheets. The 'reflection' component was somewhat lacking, but after giving my feedback and sharing student exemplars, my kids proved to be very thoughtful. At the start of each morning, we had a class discussion about what students did for home'work' the evening before, their successes and next steps. My students were excited to share, and in so doing, motivated one another to continue their quests for more balanced lifestyles. There was no stress, and a general feeling of accomplishment: the camaraderie that comes with working toward a common goal.

During week two of the trial, most of my students took ownership of their home'work' and continued to complete it and now tracked it on their own! Although time was limited, my students still came in each day wanting to share what they had accomplished the evening before. At the conclusion of the trial in week two, 80% of my students brought back their home'work' tracking sheets without prompting or reminders! They *wanted* to hand them in to me.

AUTHOR COMMENT

We simply love the idea of "home'share'" described by Peter. Considering "work" a part of the sharing process, reshapes how we perceive the time families are asked to spend with our learners after school, and also bridges the gap between play and learning.

At the end of the two weeks, I elicited parent feedback and collected and reviewed all student tracking sheets. My takeaways from the home'work' trial? I'll definitely continue this with my new grade 5/6 class in September. Importantly, I'll also continue with my home'share' initiative, as I have had nothing but success with this type of after-school activity. One thing is for certain: In my classroom, "traditional homework" has become a thing of the past.

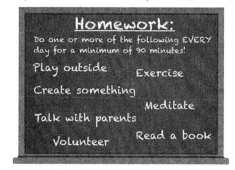

Dear Parents/Guardians,

June 13, 2016

In addition to our tradition Home'share', for the last two weeks of school, I am hoping your child will complete home'work' for a minimum of 90 minutes a day, INCLUDING weekends! Please refer to the Homework Board below to see the different options that I have suggested for your child! I am also providing a checklist for your child to track his/her Home'work' completion. Upon completing the sheet, your child is encouraged to reflect on his/her Home'work'. They may wish to write about trends that they noticed, successes, challenges, new things they learned and goals they have for the following week.

I have written a blog post about my idea and am hoping you will provide me with your initial reaction, feedback and suggestions as I truly value input, from you, the parents and guardians of my students. I will send out a "Remind" notification this evening with a short questionnaire, should you wish to fill it in. In two weeks, I'll send out another questionnaire for additional input and suggestions.

As always,

Thank you!

Peter

Homework:

Do one or more of the following EVERY day for a minimum of 90 minutes!

Play outside   Exercise

Create something

Meditate

Talk with parents

Volunteer   Read a book

Homework doesn't have to be onerous; it can be enjoyable and *should* be. It can provide a fantastic opportunity for students to really allow their learning to sink in and to celebrate time at home with their families, doing activities that make sense for everyone. It's antiquated to think that the work we send home should fit in a backpack and make up for learning that didn't get done during class hours. Given the myriad pressures faced by today's students, it's our job to make sure they get the time they need to have fun and reflect on the day's learning, not to insert additional tasks into their already busy lives.

HACK 6

SPARK CURIOSITY
BEFORE THE LESSON

Make connections that generate interest in learning

"I have no special talents. I am only passionately curious."
—ALBERT EINSTEIN

THE PROBLEM: HOMEWORK IS ALWAYS
GIVEN IN THE SAME SEQUENCE

WHEN HOMEWORK BECOMES the class work that isn't completed during the day, there is no impetus beyond compliance to engage with the assignment in a meaningful way. Some teachers use homework exclusively as a means of practicing skills taught in class, overlooking potential opportunities to spark excitement about learning. When these are the primary reason for designing homework, we don't allow students to use their imaginations in ways that could potentially enrich their learning in class.

Because we want to engage students' interests and love of learning, we need to avoid these situations:

- Sequencing in which we assign work is often dictated by the scope of the content. The pacing calendar tells us what has to be taught and when, and can feel like a pair of handcuffs in terms of what is expected in and out of the classroom.

- Homework that just reviews class work is redundant for students who have already mastered the day's learning. In drilling content, such repetition also reduces interest in the material.

- Offering one sequence for learning turns students off, especially if it is only practice after a lesson has been taught.

THE HACK: SPARK CURIOSITY BEFORE THE LESSON

Too often we assign traditional homework so that students will practice what they have learned in class, but this is not the only way to help students learn. We need to activate the curiosity that resides in all learners. Sometimes, predictive or anticipatory activities get students wondering about something they haven't learned yet.

WHAT YOU CAN DO TOMORROW

- **Compile a list of students' interests.** When making choices about sequencing, evaluate which anticipatory activities will spark the most interest. Compile student information the old fashioned way by asking them to write their interests on pieces of paper, or have a classroom discussion, with a class recorder writing down what is shared. You can even create a Google Form for more reticent students who do not feel comfortable participating in other ways. If you discover a student has an interest in magic, you might place a top hat and wand on the front table, to pique interest in what you're about to launch in the next unit.

- **Audit upcoming lessons.** If you are required to write lesson plans, you may want to look at the units you have already composed and consider where opportunities to spark activity exist. Ask yourself, where would this be appropriate? What am I trying to achieve? Where might there be a lull that calls for a "spark activity," (something that builds curiosity quickly) to increase engagement with the content? Then, in light of the answers to these questions, re-evaluate the scope and sequence of your lesson plans.

- **Present preliminary activities and assess without a test.** Start to drop hints about future lessons, with the goal of getting students to explore upcoming material outside of class. Give students enough to get excited but not enough to satiate their curiosity; interest must be piqued but not quenched. Consider activities like putting a sealed box on a desk and engaging students in a round of 20 questions to figure out what is in the box. The contents of the box should somehow relate to future lessons, so as to get students thinking about a particular theme or concept they are about to learn.

A BLUEPRINT FOR FULL IMPLEMENTATION

Step 1: Explore where anticipatory activities make sense.

One activity that extends beyond "What You Can Do Tomorrow" is reviewing curriculum maps to insert anticipatory activities where appropriate, mixing up learning in such a way that will entice students into the unit focus. We certainly don't want to overuse this method; just like with any other activity or protocol, we risk losing its luster. Assessing the content, scope, and pace of learning, and making room for the intermittent insertion of preview activities, is the most effective way forward. Spend time evaluating the curriculum and pacing maps with grade-level teams and content-area teams—depending on the age of students—to implement the best curricular progression over the course of the year.

Step 2: Trigger curiosity with kernels of the unknown.

Anticipation guides are great for building excitement about a topic as well as presenting the goals of an entire unit at the very beginning. Triggering curiosity can be as simple as creating a series of agree/disagree statements that ask students to make judgment calls connecting prior knowledge with upcoming information.

Another strategy is encouraging students to come up with questions of their own about the new material they will be exploring. Spend class time teaching students to pose their own guiding questions. Collaborative groups can follow their curiosity to generate a list of questions around the unit of study. The questions can be refined to ensure they are open-ended and not closed-ended in nature, resulting in simple facts easily found anywhere. We want these questions to be broad ranged, offering multiple potential answers. In addition to heightening interest, it supports cooperative learning among students.

Step 3: Direct students to self-select questions for research.

After students have collaboratively generated questions, have each student select a different question he or she is interested in exploring. Because they were able to articulate details that truly triggered their curiosity, students will be inspired to research answers to these questions. This process can include asking family members, reading online, reviewing texts, or any other resources the students can access to help scratch the curiosity itch. When each member of a team brings a different focus, it supports a collaborative approach and shifts the locus of control from the teacher to the students.

Step 4: Link individual learning to make meaning.

Once each student has gathered information on his/her question, allow time in class to share the discoveries. Be sure they are identifying where there is overlap so they connect each piece of information to the overall study. Providing these multiple perspectives on the same topic gives students the opportunity to see how their individual piece relates to other pieces of evidence. This process inspires students to explore their own interests and sets up an environment for learning that makes every child a contributing member. The overall summaries that students create serve as background knowledge as the unit progresses.

Step 5: Revisit student inquiry throughout the unit.

When students share their summaries, display them in a place that will allow everyone to access their beginning thoughts. If there are misconceptions, leave them there. Use this information to frame your future lessons, encouraging students to revisit their initial thinking and revise as they develop clarity around the content. Teaching students to think metacognitively creates visible learning that they can use while exploring new material throughout their lives.

OVERCOMING PUSHBACK

We're often compelled to use homework to evaluate what students learned in class that day, or to get students to review and practice the material. Some may claim that this is the best use of at-home learning time, opposing proposals to shift the traditional learning sequence. You will be able to overcome such pushback with the following responses:

How can homework be about something students know nothing about? We often don't give students enough credit. In this YouTube world we live in, it's naive to think that kids can't gather information about something we haven't covered. They really only need the correct spelling of a concept to Google it and/or find videos about it. When we allow students to approach a topic before we do so in class, they grow curious, follow their own lines of inquiry, and practice independence skills.

Students need to use home time for practice. Although it's true that some students need additional time for practice at home, this isn't the case for all students. Even the kids who require practice will benefit from approaching learning from a different angle. Furthermore, practice shouldn't always mimic what has been done in class. We want to push students to apply ideas, skills, and concepts to new learning, developing the depth of their content understanding as well as their analytical abilities. Thus, even if practice is necessary, it can be offered not just for old, but also new concepts. Practice can make perfect, but practice doesn't look the same for every child.

Curiosity doesn't have a place in homework; it should be reserved for other activities. This is just crazy-pants! Creating interest should be a primary goal of teaching. Our job as educators is to make learning fun so that students become adults who are lifelong learners; curiosity plays a huge role in this. As inquisitive adults, we eagerly search for information until our curiosity is satisfied.

THE HACK IN ACTION

Justin Birckbichler is a fourth-grade teacher at Stafford County Public Schools in Virginia and a Google for Education Certified Innovator. He has been teaching for three years. Justin describes how he sparks learning outside the classroom to ignite engagement before the lesson, which leads to students coming to class eager to learn even more.

Justin's Story

In my fourth-grade classroom, engaging in the content at home often precedes the lesson. I prefer to use home learning time as a way to spark my students' interest or front-load them with information, rather than as a vehicle to practice in-class work. This type of anticipatory homework takes many different forms, some of them technology-based and others based on student interactions with the world and people around them.

We flip our classroom for math and I use that to introduce concepts ahead of time. More important, I have compiled a list of my students' various interests (based on Hack 10 in *Hacking Education*) and use this information to make videos that compel and engage them. For example, I knew one student loved softball but hated learning new math concepts. In introducing the subject of long division, I created a video depicting a scenario in which a softball team had to divide new gloves amongst its members. When this student returned to school the next morning, she was excited to learn more about long division.

It's not always a video that generates curiosity and wonder in my students. For my state's standards, students must understand US

Customary Units and metric measurements in mass, length, and capacity. Before students left for the day, I gave them each a list of things to find around their homes, providing them with non-traditional measurement instructions. Rather than saying, "Find something that is an inch long," I told them to find something about the size of the middle knuckle on their fingers. The students returned the next morning, eager to share what they had unearthed for each measurement. Many students found pencil cap erasers, while one student shared that his kitten's paw was the same size. This activity led into our measurement unit, meaning that each student had his/her very own benchmark measurement to apply to US Customary and metric measurements.

> **AUTHOR COMMENT**
>
> Like the Blueprint and What You Can Do Tomorrow sections, Justin highlights the importance of using student interests to incite curiosity and engage students beyond the school day. This is essential for keeping learning going 24-7.

I suggest students visit various locations with their families over the weekends (especially over the holidays or school breaks). The Civil War is a huge component of my curriculum and my students are fortunate enough to live in a state with hundreds of battlefields. Many of the battles we study are within a 90-minute drive from our school, so I'll tell parents and students that it would be good to take a family trip to the battlefield ahead of its appearance in our curriculum. I'll highlight specific areas of the visitors' center or battlefield that they should visit, and suggest tours to join.

For students who may not be able to make the trip, I will visit the location myself and send pictures and messages directly to students and their parents through a messaging app, Google Classroom, Facebook, and Twitter. This type of communication ensures that all students are able to experience the "pre-homework" and are ready to learn!

Another important era in my curriculum is the end of legal segregation. I knew that many of my students' grandparents were alive during the beginnings of integration, so I asked my students to call or visit their grandparents and ask them what they knew about Massive Resistance and/or what school was like for them in the 1950s and 1960s. After talking with their grandparents, my students were shocked to hear that schools shut down for a while! They were hungry to learn more, which helped me transition into the next unit.

AUTHOR COMMENT

The examples provided by Justin are an easy way to help parents connect with kids, encouraging them to broaden their learning beyond the classroom. Since Starr loves taking her son Logan to historical sites to experience actual history, Logan is later able to link these trips with his mom back to the learning that happens in school.

Prompting lesson reflection at home often serves as an effective point of entry into a unit, especially if assignments are concrete and relevant. Simply memorizing that a nine-sided shape is called a nonagon is boring and disconnected, but assigning students to find a nonagon at home or even in nature creates a culture of wonder, curiosity, and adventure.

Learning doesn't always happen in the traditional order, and when crafting lessons, we need to assess what sequence will improve instruction and engage students. Remember, impactful out-of-school activities are great precursors to learning, helping parents get involved in the education of their kids while helping students connect classroom material to family relationships, meaningful exploration outside of school, and to their everyday lives.

Simple choices about how and when we approach material can determine whether students are engaged. Anticipatory activities inspire students to approach learning in a meaningful way—even outside of school.

HACK 7

USE THE DIGITAL PLAYGROUND

Harness social media for learning

"We cannot solve our problems with the same
thinking we used when we created them."
—ALBERT EINSTEIN

THE PROBLEM: SCHOOLS HAVEN'T
CHANGED WITH THE TIMES

MOST STUDENTS SPEND recreational time on their personal devices—phones, laptops, and tablets—often instead of doing their homework. School systems infringe on this personal time and space, ignoring the inclinations of students by expecting them to do work the old fashioned way: in a notebook or on a worksheet with a pencil. It's a double-whammy—first, students are not interested in content and then they are turned off by the manner in which they must complete the assignment. We have to stop avoiding the digital shift and start embracing technology, as it is vital to how today's students learn in school, but even more so at home.

Since we can't and shouldn't avoid the digital trends in learning and work, we need to address and shift these views about learning with technology:

- With social media viewed as an enemy of or escape from learning, schools treat sites like Facebook and Twitter as a threat to sound practice. Some schools even block social media and have policies against students using it at school.

- Students aren't learning how to properly use new social outlets, and as a result, are abusing them, failing to act like good digital citizens and bullying each other online.

- The pen-and-paper expectation for homework no longer reflects today's reality. Instead of expecting a whole generation of kids to change, perhaps it's time the system does.

THE HACK: USE THE DIGITAL PLAYGROUND

Students now live in a digital world. Whether using Snapchat, Instagram, or Facetime, students communicate in a way most adults didn't at a young age. Rather than force students to approach education the way adults always have, schools must meet them where they are, integrating technology and social media into learning both in and outside of the classroom to further digital skills that will be carried with them in the future once they are done with school.

Teachers and families should recognize the promise in the technology to which students naturally gravitate. With students already adept on a range of devices, school systems can harness the power of technology and begin to teach students 21st century skills that will serve them personally and academically. Since most students are not maximizing the learning potential of their devices, they must be taught how and when to use them for the purpose of learning by having it modeled first in school and then used effectively outside of the classroom.

To learn more about working in this digital playground, check out Hacks 5 and 9 in *Hacking Education* by Mark Barnes and Jennifer Gonzalez.

WHAT YOU CAN DO TOMORROW

- **Define digital footprint with younger students**. In the ever-growing digital world, our "footprints" are more visible and far-reaching than most of us realize. Students need to learn early about the magnitude of their digital choices. Begin these conversations in elementary school. Starting tomorrow, talk about what students post, where they post, how they share, and how their engagement with the digital world impacts their lives. These classroom exchanges will help you understand what you need to teach both younger and older students moving forward. Through these conversations about students' digital presences, you will find out which applications they are using, allowing you to adjust to meet them where they are and adjust conversations appropriately to those forums.

- **Communicate electronically.** One super easy thing you can do is to start allowing students to submit work electronically. If your school isn't a Google school yet, start by accepting work via email. If you are a Google school, Google Docs and associated applications offer a variety of sharing choices, generating a valuable paper trail that is stored in the cloud. No more worries about lost papers. For younger students, this could be a great way to get parents involved as early as tomorrow, especially if students don't have their own emails yet. Parents can then review work with their child/children and send the work on behalf of their child/children until the child/children are old enough to have email accounts of their own.

- **Fetch a list of students' favorite apps.** This is something that takes a few minutes but will pay off immediately. Once you are aware of the apps students use, get to know them yourself and explore them for educational purposes. When kids understand how to use these apps for learning and not just for fun, they can participate in teaching lunch and learns, as well as take leadership roles in the classroom; you can ask kids, for example, to lead a lesson about an app they suggested. Exposing students to ways apps keep them connected and assist with learning opens the door to them using these 21st century tools for their learning at home. The more we fill their toolboxes, the more resources they have to explore their interests and extend lessons beyond the classroom. It may be worthwhile to get parents to sign off on applications for younger students, so that they are kept in the loop about their children's interactions with the digital world and know what to expect in regard to data usage.

- **Survey the class about the devices they use and how they use them.** Knowing how many of your students are mobile and using tablets and how many are on desktop or laptop computers will be important for knowing how students will be submitting learning activities or communicating. Do the devices they use influence how flexible they are in what they are doing? These are some questions you'll need to consider, along with the age of your students and the level of access they have when alone and/or with a parent. If students don't have access to technology, this will also be an opportunity to discuss what they can do at home instead that will keep learning continuous. Whether recommending the use of a local library or lending the technology to students if that is possible, keeping in contact with parents to better support home learning is necessary. Technology is only one tool to assist in learning and the absence of it doesn't mean that learning can't be done. Provide alternatives in these situations, like using a notebook or a folder, and then allotting for time in class for documents or assignments to be typed. A local public library is a resource for Internet use or for research books if students cannot take the classroom textbooks home.

- **Talk to colleagues informally about how they are using technology.** When we want learning to stick, it helps that we aren't working alone. So start some informal discussions with colleagues about how they are using technology both in and out of the classroom. These conversations can be springboards for collaboration or entry points for moving forward in the learning process on behalf of students and parents. Exchanges with colleagues produce new information about what is working in other spaces and what hasn't worked. Always approach from a place of learning and not a place of knowing, so that you're welcoming ideas rather than just preaching. This can also be a great way to align expectations outside of school around social media in more than one class.

A BLUEPRINT FOR FULL IMPLEMENTATION

Step 1: Review guidelines of use with students.

Students must know more than just that a policy exists; they must understand why it is in place and how best to abide by it. Once they know why and how to use the guidelines, classes can freely employ digital tools to make learning public either within the closed online groups (for younger students) or open to everyone on the Internet. Use class time to rewrite guidelines in child-friendly language for younger students and keep these guidelines hanging somewhere in the classroom. Try to consistently reference the guidelines as a reminder to students. If any challenges should arise, incorporate the guidelines into the conversation that must be had with the student and parents.

Step 2: Piggyback on your school and/or district regulations for social media use at home.

As the times change, almost every school district is changing with them by adopting social media regulations that both keep students safe and create dialogue about learning in this new forum. Now that you've reviewed your school's policy, your classroom activities should align with these regulations. Social media is a great place to start sharing success stories that help open up your district to a less restrictive social media environment.

Since social media policies exist to keep students safe and to build community, it is important to help parents understand these policies so they can support their children at home in using these guidelines correctly. Teach students to turnkey this information to their parents so that the same appropriate use is happening in the home. Continued practice and support with parents will help to develop community and exposure to the school's success stories.

Step 3: Model and practice appropriate behaviors on social media.

Depending on the age of students, both open and closed social media platforms can be used. For younger students, closed platforms like Edmodo, Meetup, or Kidblog help students practice good digital citizenship in class. For older students, use Twitter or Google Communities as a way to backchannel discussions both in and out of class. The teacher should moderate these conversations until students grasp the purpose of the activity and are able to fully participate on their own. A class hashtag like #WJPSaplit, #WJPSnews, or #SCSPLN serves as an additional learning resource for students and parents. Additionally having these class hashtags makes learning visible and available from home in the form it took during the school day. The students can review the learning as it happened in school and use the same behavior in their own time.

To ensure that students truly understand how to participate in digital forums, make sure to break down what this participation should look like. Consider running extra help sessions on Twitter or Google Plus where students can continue the learning with classmates and their parents from home.

For elementary students, try creating a Twitter wall, where kids write tweets about outside learning on construction paper and hang them publicly. Teach students about the appropriate use of tweets, and what character limitations are. Remind them to use the class hashtags. Give them ample time to practice in class before you invite them to use these resources outside of school, like Jennifer Scheffer suggests in her Hack in Action.

Step 4: Monitor social spaces to ensure that students are using them appropriately.

When showing kids how to use these spaces, you must at first be involved in monitoring what is going on. Inappropriate use is an opportunity for a teachable moment, and such moments form the basis for a lifetime of proper usage. Teachers have the platform to shape how students engage with digital spaces both in and out of school, and the way we shape student usage must be done with care. In regard to younger students, make sure they can be upstanders and help point out the need for discussion in areas where they might inadvertently misuse or bully each other online.

Jump into digital exchanges and model how to moderate or shut down a potentially harmful situation. For example, if a student suggests that a post is "stupid" and doesn't add anything meaningful in a comment, the teacher can intervene, requesting additional information, asking clarifying questions, reminding the group that "stupid" isn't a constructive way of disagreeing, and providing an alternative sentence starter for disagreement, such as "I don't agree because ____" or "This doesn't support my beliefs because _____. " The students will quickly learn that it is okay to disagree, but they need to provide reasons and the comment must move the conversation forward.

Once class time is spent in the forums together, teachers have more confidence in how students use them outside of school, helping kids to interact without bullying behavior, and knowing what to do if something oversteps the boundary of appropriate comments. Since the access will be less monitored, at least immediately at home, students must know how to de-escalate potentially challenging situations to shut them down, rather than engage in them and making them worse.

Step 5: If you don't know how to use different apps that students are using, ask students to lead lunch and learn sessions.

We sometimes have to put our pride away when we teach; not knowing something can be a real strength when we empower students to share what they know. A great way to learn about new apps is to allow students to present them in class. Potential options include the creation of screencast tutorials, to be kept in a virtual library for student and teacher use, and student lunch and learn presentations on the apps, with recordings of the sessions available for interested parties. This way, students who can't participate in person have access to the information later. Students are always excited to disclose what they know, and regardless of age, want to help each other. Students also love when teachers learn from them, so the exchange is mutually beneficial.

OVERCOMING PUSHBACK

Since social media began playing a prominent role in student and teacher lives, the question of its academic viability has become a hot topic. There will always be folks who fail to see the value of meeting kids where they are with technology and social media, but here are some ways you can combat pushback:

Social media has no place in the learning process in or out of school. Many folks will say that social media is not appropriate for school because it is a distraction and there is nothing educational about the space. Social media, however, has the power to make the world a much smaller, more connected place. This is a medium with which students are *already* engaging, and often not for the best purposes, so teach them to use it effectively. Pretending that they aren't using the different platforms and communicating both appropriately and inappropriately is putting your head in the sand. In order to ensure students make the most of these environments and stay safe while using them, they MUST be shown how to do so, both through teacher modeling and opportunities to practice. And as far as distraction goes, if the lesson isn't engaging, students will find ways to be distracted with or without social media. Stop blaming the devices and a take a deeper look at what is being taught in the learning space.

Our job description doesn't include "social media police." Agreed that you aren't the social media police, but if you saw a child bullying another child on the playground, you'd likely stop it. This is no different. Teaching children to behave in a mature and seemly manner is part of our jobs, so it is important to go to the playgrounds where students play to ensure that they are doing so safely and appropriately. We would never take kids to an unsupervised location and leave them alone, with no instruction, so why should that happen with social media? It's easy enough to be someone who oversees social media use without it dominating the job.

"But I'm not active on social media." So now is as good a time as any to start. Social media is an excellent tool for networking and researching. Sign up for a free Twitter account for professional usage that you can share with students and model what it means to be a good digital citizen. Once you get your handle up and running, demonstrate for students in class how to have conversations online with the specific goal of extending those conversations beyond the classroom at home. Being active on Twitter offers a way for students to collaborate about class learning or a way to offer extra help where needed at home.

For younger students, start a class account and post to it on behalf of the students, going low-tech in class—writing tweets or other posts out on paper first and then posting the papers on the wall to make the "tweets" visible. Examine Figure 7.1 for an example of how one teacher executed this. By creating this space online, students have a resource to revisit at home while extending learning beyond the day.

Figure 7.1

THE HACK IN ACTION

Sharing her expertise in creating meaningful home learning with Twitter is Jennifer L. Scheffer, M.Ed., who facilitated a student-run Help Desk program for three years, and worked as a technology integration specialist for Burlington Public Schools in New Hampshire. In her Hack in Action, Jennifer shares how she brought Twitter into her lab to extend learning beyond the school day.

Jennifer's Story

While serving as the facilitator of the student-run Help Desk at Burlington High School, one of my goals was to help students leverage social media tools to build their professional networks, develop a positive digital footprint, and emerge as digital role models for their peers both locally and globally. This was accomplished by integrating Twitter into the curriculum.

My students were already active users of Twitter, but were employing the tool for personal rather than professional reasons. To reach my curriculum goal of teaching students how to collaborate with others through digital tools, I introduced them to the concept of Twitter chats. I provided concrete examples of how educators were using Twitter and educational hashtags and taught students the mechanics of Twitter chats, giving them a clear understanding of how their own engagement with Twitter could evolve from personal use to a more meaningful method of digital communication with peers and adults. After showing my students the question and answer structure of a professional Twitter chat, I then had them create their own Twitter chat discussion topic and unique hashtag. This is when the hashtag #techteamMA was born.

In the fall of 2013, I organized a live Google Hangout On Air with several student-run technology teams from Massachusetts. During this video call, students described the structures of their respective teams and the way in which they served their 1:1 or BYOD learning communities. It was a rich discussion and once it was over, Kerry Gallagher, former history teacher turned digital learning coach, suggested that the students continue the conversation on a monthly basis through Twitter. Every adult facilitator in that video call agreed that a student-led Twitter chat would be an excellent way to maintain and grow the connections our students had established. Several months later, I decided to take the leap and organize the first student-led Twitter chat.

AUTHOR COMMENT

Meeting students where they are but shifting the focus from personal to professional use of the tool — Jenn's Hack in Action — is a goal many of us share. As mentioned earlier, too often we expect students to come to us and we end up failing when they refuse to do so. Instead we must figure out where they are and meet them there.

The first task was to create a unique hashtag so students could follow and keep up with the conversation. That's when Nathan Rippin, Burlington High School Class of 2015, suggested #techteamMA. The hashtag was officially adopted. The next several tasks included: developing the Twitter chat topic and questions, selecting two student moderators to lead the chat, creating a Google Doc with the chat questions and timing of each question, and promoting the chat across social networks to increase participation. The Google Doc was shared with all of the tech teams that were planning to be involved. I next showed my students how to use the tool Tweetdeck to schedule their Tweets in advance and how to organize their Twitter stream in order to keep up with and participate in the live chat. After developing the questions for the chat (there were six questions), my students and I discussed how to best answer each question in the form of a Tweet.

Students quickly realized how challenging it was to answer a complex question in only 140 characters and this became an excellent opportunity for them to hone their writing skills. Students were forced to think critically about their responses and craft a Tweet that had substance. Students completed this task, and scheduled their Tweets—based on the timing of each question—via Tweetdeck during class time. Their participation in the live chat, however, occurred outside of class. The live Twitter chat was what one would label, by traditional standards, "homework."

> **AUTHOR**
> COMMENT
>
> Implementing a mixture of tools that demonstrate the value of technology in a real setting is a great way to align learning outside of school with career and college goals. The story of Jenn's students highlights the different means of communicating via technology, like Twitter, Google Hangouts, and Google Docs. The student-led chat also shows how collaboration breeds more learning throughout the day in a fluid and natural way both in and out of school.

I was not surprised in the least that all of my students participated in the live chat (it ran from 7:00-8:00 p.m. EST). When they returned to class the next day, they were excited about the conversation and the connections they had made with other students from across the state. This assignment had meaning, was relevant to students' lives, and gave them a sense of empowerment, leadership, and confidence that traditional homework could not.

The Twitter chat became a monthly collaborative effort between my students and other student tech teams, giving all involved a strong understanding of how to use Twitter professionally and responsibly. I had accomplished what I set out to do and was incredibly proud of the digital role models my students had become.

As a result of this assignment, my students quickly realized that they could demonstrate their aptitude for digital citizenship through Twitter. Many of them took the initiative to make connections with colleges and industry professionals. Students realized that Twitter could help them accomplish their academic and professional goals. As their facilitator, this was incredibly rewarding.

What started as a one-hour Twitter chat—a homework assignment—morphed into an activity that was truly life changing for several of my students. For any teacher out there who is seeking to change his/her approach to homework, consider employing Twitter in a similar manner. Homework doesn't have to be assigned daily for students to achieve mastery of the curriculum learning objectives. A monthly assignment, similar to the one I have described, is more meaningful than a ho-hum worksheet.

With proper planning and instruction, your students can also have a transformative experience that begins with 140 characters. Your willingness as an educator to take a strategic risk and integrate a digital communication tool into the curriculum can grow into a wealth of learning opportunities with more expansive social media tools like blogging platforms.

Since students are already using technology and social media to communicate with each other and explore the world we live in, it's necessary for schools to get on board. Bringing social media like Twitter into play aligns with student interests and orients the time spent in digital spaces toward learning rather than just socializing.

Creating a balance of valuable relationship-building time and learning in and out of school is essential to helping students function well in this digital time. Social media helps to marry the technology with the face-to-face experiences we encounter and helps develop interpersonal skills and literacy skills at the same time. Incorporating online chats or digital portfolios into our plans for both in- and out-of-class learning provides families and students with a level of transparency and connection that only deepens the learning experience.

HACK 8

AMPLIFY STUDENT VOICE

Incorporate choice in how kids learn at home

*"I never teach my pupils. I only attempt to provide
the conditions in which they can learn."*
—ALBERT EINSTEIN

THE PROBLEM: STUDENTS DON'T HAVE A
SAY IN WHAT AND HOW THEY LEARN

EDUCATION GENERALLY USES a top-down model, ignoring the
most important voice—the student's. Administrators make
choices about policy that don't embrace the teacher voice and then
teachers make choices without hearing the student voice. We tend
to rob students of decisions about their education and tell them
what must be done, forcing them into compliance.

If education is truly about students, however, we must let students
take ownership. The game of compliance doesn't inspire learning

but quashes it, making critical thinking harder down the road. We want to make sure we take the opportunity to amplify student voice because:

- The less ownership we give students, the less they have the ability to think for themselves. They develop excessive concern for learning the "right" way, inferring that there is only one right way to learn. In reality, we have students with a variety of backgrounds and strengths, each one requiring something different. We can't lump them together and decide that one approach works for all.

- Learning should be a partnership, with the learner's needs central to decision-making. The expression of discontent in the form of non-compliance (not doing the work or copying someone else's) is an outcome of not involving students in the decision-making process.

- When we don't allow students to have a say, the purpose of the home learning is often unclear. It seems meaningless. Some students will follow teacher directions mindlessly but others won't. This dynamic jeopardizes the learning process.

THE HACK: AMPLIFY STUDENT VOICE; GIVE KIDS CHOICE

Once students understand what quality learning looks like both in and out of school, we can start involving them in decision-making, helping them make meaningful choices that deepen their learning. In this way, students are responsible for and invested in what they do. Since the work was their choice to begin with, the motivation to complete it is intrinsic.

Students must have some say about what they learn and how they learn it, especially when it happens at home. When given the opportunity to make choices about home learning, most students develop sound options; sometimes even better ones than teachers. If we want learning to extend beyond the day, we must offer students the chance to create learning on their own.

WHAT YOU CAN DO TOMORROW

- **Debate what quality looks like.** The more students are engaged in discussions about successful learning, the better you are able to understand their perceptions of learning and what they need to succeed. Listening to students' ideas about homework will help you give more effective assignments. Additionally, teachers can offer an exemplar and do a jigsaw in class, evaluating different assignments for home and then developing a checklist of the qualities that make it meaningful from the model they are examining. This way, the list comes directly from student thoughts and engagement.

- **Teach students to design their own learning opportunities.** Instead of only one assignment for home, offer a "choose your own adventure" option in which students decide how to demonstrate their knowledge but still fulfill learning objectives. It's good to have students get ideas approved at first, which also gives teachers the opportunity to provide immediate feedback on what students come up with. If the students do a great job (which they often do), then offer student ideas to the whole class as options for the future. Saying yes is much more gratifying than saying no.

- **Accept a variety of submissions.** Perhaps one of the simplest things we can do is offer students a choice as to how the work they do at home gets submitted. Instead of providing only a worksheet or asking for work to be written in a Google Doc, take student preference into account when deciding on the "how." If students feel more comfortable undertaking the work in a certain medium, it's very easy for you to let them do so. Too often we say no as a function of habit, because we want to control the way everything looks and make sure students comply. This attitude turns some students off and even constitutes a missed opportunity for learning. So try to stay open when a student makes a suggestion.

A BLUEPRINT FOR FULL IMPLEMENTATION

Step 1: Dissect the design process.

In order for this all to work, students must fully understand how to create a meaningful home learning experience. Spend time in class teaching the backward planning method, evaluating what you want the outcome to be.

Dissect the process, allowing students to practice in class. One way to do this is to divide students into small groups to look at an assignment. Ask them to annotate the assignment and try to figure out the "point" of it. Once they can do this, ask them to generate a new assignment that seeks to attain the same learning outcomes as the original. Either allow for multiple iterations of the assignment or have the class determine which one of the student samples should be the basis for an actual assignment. Over time, this practice will become a part of classroom culture, as will students' expectations of participating in the development of how they extend their thinking at home and other learning experiences.

Step 2: Furnish feedback on home learning ideas.

As students work on developing new ideas for activities outside of class, it is vital that teachers and peers provide specific feedback on student proposals. Students need to know if they are headed in the right direction. If they aren't, they need to be redirected as quickly as possible. Teachers can give feedback in a number of ways: set up a system in which peer leaders in each group are responsible for feedback, meet with small groups in class so as to not create additional work outside of class, or have students submit ideas via Google Docs and provide feedback on the documents directly. You can learn more about ways to get students involved as peer reviewers in *Empower Students to Give Feedback: Teaching Students to Provide Effective Peer Feedback*, in which Starr gives detailed advice on how to construct these systems.

Step 3: Involve parents in the process.

Sometimes learning doesn't have to come from school. Parents may encounter opportunities outside of the classroom that meaningfully advance student learning. If you maintain an open line with parents, they can supplement classroom learning with family learning, like when cooking a family meal or putting together a new bookshelf. Always keep communication channels open; we'll take a closer look at teaming up with families in Hack 9. These connections may wind up being beneficial for the whole class.

Step 4: Practice saying "yes" instead of "no." Sometimes the most valuable lessons come from ideas that don't work out.

It's easy enough to say no to students if you hear something different than what you want or expect, such as when you already have an idea planned. Unfortunately, this may be a knee-jerk reaction. So it's important to pause and take in what the student is suggesting. Really listen to him/her. Ask questions about alignment with learning objectives and what the new homework will look like. It doesn't need to be an interrogation but rather clarification and follow-up questions. Sometimes it's a good idea to let students follow their own paths, even if you suspect it won't work out the way they plan. Failure serves as a wonderful learning experience in itself.

Step 5: Reflect on choices and development as a part of the process.

Reflection is key to the learning process. Although reflection may not need to be documented and/or submitted like homework, it's necessary to make it a conscious part of the metacognitive journey. We should encourage students to reflect in ways that work for them and that will provide the best returns for time spent. Some may enjoy writing publicly on a blog or privately in a journal. Some may like to talk, or Vox with themselves. Some may enjoy vlogging or just having conversations with friends about learning. Ultimately, we'd like students to develop the habit of documenting their thinking processes, but this should be organic documentation and not forced, as the latter can ruin opportunities for authentic growth. Try not to limit kids to what works for you as a teacher. Offer suggestions, but be okay if they don't take them.

Step 6: Foster sharing of ideas.

Great ideas deserve to be shared, and so does the learning that comes from them. If a student has an idea worth sharing, make time in class to allow him/her to do so. Potential sharing options include gallery walks for multiple ideas at once, thereby generating full class conversations; short presentations; or having students create multimedia experiences to recount their learning. Any time we highlight or showcase brilliant student work, we show kids that their ideas matter. Do more of this in school and don't only focus on the critical/constructive/negative feedback that often plays too much of a crucial role in students' lives.

Step 7: Celebrate student choices and adopt new ideas (always make sure to give them credit).

If what students have created is replicable, then it should be replicated. What an amazing legacy for students if one of their homework ideas ends up in the curriculum for future classes. Always ask permission from students to share their ideas and give credit when using their ideas in the future. For example, if one student develops a research project around solving a local problem as suggested in Don Wettrick's Hack in Action, why not work with that student to track the steps so other students can replicate the process to solve other problems? Once the students see the success one student has had, they will be challenged to try to solve problems that are more personally pressing for each of them.

One other example is to coordinate feature projects that incorporate students' passions. We know that when interest is high students will create their own inquiry around a topic. Ask them to find experts in the field to talk to for real-world connections rather than asking them to do research only online or in books. Once they do the research and write or develop their multimedia project, display it on the student media outlet or within the school so that more students and community members have access to the excellent learning. Having students share their hard work and even speak about it can inspire other students to do the same.

OVERCOMING PUSHBACK

Folks who favor the traditional will say that students aren't capable of coming up with comparably effective and rigorous homework ideas. They will insist that it's a teacher's job to design and determine the outcomes of learning. However, when we offer students the chance to get involved with planning how to deepen or extend their learning, their proposals often surprise even the biggest naysayers.

Students won't come up with sufficiently rigorous activities. Yes, there may be students who don't know how to seek out or express their interests, and some may compensate by taking "the easy way out." Kids are inherently curious. If we know what they like and have a decent relationship with them, it's simple to engage students in a dialogue that leads to meaningful activities.

Some students may require scaffolds, but this doesn't mean that they are incapable of generating challenging ideas for learning. Know your students and put plans in place that will best facilitate their success. Don't be afraid to have different accountability measures, such as a journal to record ideas in writing, for more challenging students. Just because there will be a required check-in doesn't make it less of their own choice, especially if we allow them to help determine the means in which they will be accountable. Once they show that they can be responsible, you can take off the training wheels.

Educators are paid to teach students how to learn. Helping students design learning activities and reflect on the impact of independent learning is more accurate. Although there will always be parents, students, and colleagues who believe that everything that happens in the classroom is the teacher's job to create, we know that the more agency we give students, the more they engage with their own learning. Einstein and others have said that it isn't the teacher's job to control the learning but rather the teacher's job to construct an environment in which optimal learning occurs. By giving students choice and voice in what and how they learn, the teacher honors each child's individual needs and embraces those differences to engender a better learning environment for all.

Kids need to know how to follow directions; they won't always have choices. We love this pushback. We hear it often, and it's important to discuss. Although there are times in our adult lives when following directions is key, knowing when to make suggestions to better the experience has always been a hallmark of the jobs we've had. We want to raise students to be innovators, capable of thinking on their own and not just mindlessly implementing instructions. How better to teach them this than to actually empower them?

THE HACK IN ACTION

Don Wettrick is the Innovation Coordinator at Noblesville High School, just outside Indianapolis, Indiana. He is the author of *Pure Genius: Building a Culture of Innovation and Taking 20% Time to the Next Level*. Wettrick has worked as a middle school and high school teacher, educational and innovation consultant, and speaker. Most important, Don works with educators, students, and entrepreneurs to bring innovation and collaborative skills into education. In this Hack in Action, Don shares how students go on research journeys of their own choosing to solve problems to better their communities.

Don's Story

I run an Innovation class at Noblesville High School, where we don't assign homework as a general rule. The class is basically a 20% time model, but instead of working on a project for 20% of the class, the class IS the students' 20% time. We felt that students needed a class period to work on things that interested them. So while we support all the foundational classes, we carved out a part of the school day to center around the student; to support what they want to learn. This could be anything, but most important it must be student-generated and focused. This is the heart of what a Genius Hour is, a time and space created specifically for the exploration of student interests and passions with the supports and resources students need to follow those curiosities.

> **AUTHOR COMMENT**
>
> We love framing research around a problem that matters to students. This form of inquiry is the truest form of learning and problem-solving that there is. It happens on so many levels: not just grand inquiries, but simple ones like finding alternatives to ingredients that aren't in the house. What a great way to teach students to solve everyday problems!

Two years ago a student in my innovation class, Jess Elliott, decided to embark on a journey that turned a "homework" research assignment into a two-year project. She had done some research on light pollution and saw that it was a major issue but received little attention. The research indicated that our night sky was causing various problems in nature, from birds flying into buildings to insomnia problems in humans. The biggest culprit was big cities—streetlights, neon signs, and security lighting—but what could be done about it?

136

In Jess's research she discovered that a lot of light pollution could be fixed by simply pointing streetlights down. Though many decorative "acorn lights" light up the sky, the energy efficient "cobra head" lenses use less energy AND light only the ground. This is where most "homework assignments" would have come to an end. There might have been an essay and poster combo, maybe even a survey, or QR code. But instead Jess decided to "think global and act local."

She reached out to local politicians, who in turn wanted her to help write a bill. This process took several months and ended up being a great learning opportunity. While I would like to say that the bill writing went well, the bill was eventually sent to a committee, where (Jess felt) it got too watered down. After seven months of ups and downs, she could have quit on this project. But Jess decided to go in another direction.

She got involved with organizations like the "International Dark Skies Association" (IDA) and started contacting members for their insights. She blogged, she networked, she persevered.

What Jess emerged with was a plan to work with land developers. She felt that enticing builders to install energy efficient street lamps would not only benefit the environment but also the financial bottom line. She is working on getting neighborhoods "Energy Star" certified for using lower wattage LED bulbs, and also for cutting down on light pollution.

AUTHOR COMMENT

We hear about these projects as very rare, special occurrences, but they should be more widespread. Start small with students, in attainable bites. Teach them how to find organizations that they can link up with. Show them who to reach out to and then get their parents involved to make it happen.

When Jess wasn't working with the land developers, she was

reaching out to universities for support. She gave presentations to university classes, gaining additional insights and establishing partnerships. She even decided to work with area elementary schools, where she would read a children's book about light pollution and what the students could do to help! All of this "homework" was student-directed, and she updated me based on the pacing and deadlines that we agreed upon.

Jess took TWO YEARS to work on the light pollution project, and it started with a "homework" assignment. An assignment to find out what she was passionate about. When we allot time for our students to discover a passion and ACT on it, magic happens.

And isn't that the point of education anyway? To learn about things YOU are curious about? I'm all about learning things "I ought to," but more excited about the things that have really sparked my interest.

Although Jess's two-year study may not be typical, as a great number of us don't have the chance to loop with students, Don's story shows us the power of choice and the power of Genius Hour. Giving students the opportunity to follow their own interests in a meaningful way on their own time, with all the support they need, increases their motivation and dedication to learning; learning isn't just for a grade or to comply with a policy, it's driven by self-interest. This is the purest form of learning, as it will stay with students throughout their lives.

As we continue to make out-of-school learning about kids and not about grades in books or compliance, offering students choice and voice in how they spend their own time cultivates a love for learning and develops essential life and critical thinking skills that will produce more functional adults. Merely prescribing what must be done is not learning. We must encourage students to find what they love to do and then seek it out in meaningful ways.

HACK 9

TEAM UP WITH FAMILIES
Model instructional strategies for parents

*"Insanity: Doing the same thing over and over
again and expecting different results."*
—ALBERT EINSTEIN

THE PROBLEM: PARENTS ARE UNDERUSED
AS PARTNERS IN EDUCATION

THE ONLY EXPERIENCE most parents have with school is when they were students themselves. Because they've had their own exposure to education, they often feel they are experts in student learning. Unfortunately, parents' perspectives are not only decades old, but based on a time when students were not digital learners; maybe even when research was conducted using a card catalog before the Internet.

Without proper communication and explanation, parents won't understand the approach that today's teachers are taking to meet the needs of 21st century learners, both in and out of school. Many parents envision a classroom as consisting of carefully aligned rows of student desks, all facing the front of the class with the teacher at the center, providing more answers than questions. They take this perspective and apply it to the home learning environment, often spoon-feeding students to get the answers without a concentration on grasping the concepts.

Failing to understand the "why" can lead to lack of support. When students hear their parents make comments like, "I don't understand how to do the new math," an us-versus-them mentality is born. Teachers are forced to defend their actions and battle the homework wars alone instead of pairing up with parents to support learning experiences both inside and outside the classroom.

Subsequently, in the absence of effective communication between stakeholders, parents feel like they must have all the right answers to be helpful. In reality, a few effective questions support student learning more than these "right answers." There are some common factors that influence how parents might view learning and drive their views on the purpose and/or need for traditional homework, such as:

- Every parent has gone through school. These experiences, positive and negative, impact how parents speak about school at home with their children.

- All parents want their child to succeed, but success is often based on right answers and not deep understanding of concepts and skills.

- As times change, the needs of students have changed. Over the years, teaching approaches have been adapted to meet these current needs, but parents are often left out of the loop on what these shifts are and why they are productive in supporting student growth both in and out of the classroom.

- Some families believe that education is initiated at school. They feel a need for a directive to come from a teacher in order for learning to be promoted. This often comes in the form of a request for homework.

THE HACK: TEAM UP WITH FAMILIES

Parents do the best they can with the information they have. We need to share the rationale behind changing approaches to education so parents can connect actions and purpose, allowing them to look at learning with a fresh perspective, revised from what they remember as students themselves. Teachers bridge this gap when they share the benefits of student choice, describing how probing questions support independence, and reinforcing that learning is 24-7 in all environments, not just paper-pencil tasks.

Seeing broader purpose and transferrable skills empowers students to be partners in education instead of bystanders. In order to help parents understand 21st century shifts in education, we can model these innovative strategies. Changing parents' conceptions of learning is an important step toward teaming with them so students extend learning opportunities everywhere. We want parents taking advantage of teachable moments even if it's not assigned from the teacher.

WHAT YOU CAN DO TOMORROW

- **Explain the why.** Just as when you sit in a PD session or staff meeting and something new or different is introduced, making you wonder about its value, parents are likely to experience this same confusion. If we don't supply an explicit rationale for our decisions about learning, unanswered questions can turn into a Facebook rant, such as, "I don't understand why my child's teacher doesn't give homework." If you've defined the why for parents, you're likely to see another parent from your class commenting on the status, explaining it this way: "Our child's teacher said she doesn't give homework because our daughter is encouraged to read for pleasure, play games with the family and explore her interests. We appreciate having a teacher who understands the benefits beyond homework."

- **Identify concepts that are often difficult for students.** Scan your unit plans for lessons that are difficult or confusing. Make a note to ramp up your communication with parents during these units to let them know that their children might struggle at first, but will eventually get it.

- **Include future learning objectives in your communication with parents.** When sending information to parents, flip the sequence in which you discuss learning in the classroom. It doesn't do much good for parents to know what you've already done in class. They can be much more helpful partners if they get a heads up on what's to come. Change your curriculum summary from "Last week we…" to "Next week we will be…" Then offer some content-specific support so that parents can engage in the learning process.

- **Practice what you preach.** Do you have parents sit and listen to you talk for an hour during parent nights? Whenever you're communicating with parents, model the style you use in the classroom: mini lessons, engagement, transitions, etc. Beware of the potential hypocrisy of saying one thing but doing another. When parents experience the benefits of accountable talk or having choice, they can more easily see the benefits they have for students, and mimic when learning opportunities present themselves at home.

- **Ask parents what they need.** Instead of predicting what you think parents want or need, create a survey and solicit their feedback. Then use it! Questions you might ask include:

  - What are some ways the school has successfully supported your child's learning?

  - In what ways have you been included as a partner in your child's education?

  - In one word, how would you describe homework?

  - If your child didn't have homework or had less than 20 minutes a night, what would your child or family do with the additional time?

  - Can you provide some examples of ways you support learning at home that we can share with other parents?

A BLUEPRINT FOR FULL IMPLEMENTATION

Step 1: Identify shifts in instructional approaches that have occurred since your students' parents were in school.

If you're a teacher who uses student talk protocols, small-group instruction, and standards-based grading, you can expect that these strategies will be unfamiliar to parents. Think of running a parent meeting like you would a classroom lesson. And consider the following questions:

- Do you have learning intentions and criteria for success?

- Are you using a gradual release model?

- Do parents have an opportunity to converse with each other so as to deepen their understanding of what you're communicating to them?

With these shifts identified, you're ready to plan opportunities for parents to experience the power of these instructional strategies. The goal is for parents to be comfortable with these teaching protocols so they will model them at home either when students need help with homework, or more important, when capitalizing on educational opportunities in their day-to-day family activities.

Step 2: Rework your curriculum night, open house, and parent information meetings.

Modeling new learning strategies is much more effective than standing at the front of the room using the same delivery model that you're trying to debunk. Provide experiences for parents that will give them both a frame of reference for how they might support students at home and a better understanding of how learning occurs in your classroom. When you have parents in the building for curriculum night, or other traditional events with high attendance, take the opportunity to demonstrate a range of instructional strategies and do a think-aloud, so they understand what you're doing and why you're doing it. Imagine a jigsaw that outlines your classroom procedures. How about a chalk talk in which parents use chart paper to silently brainstorm ways to support reading and math at home, then gallery walk through the room to read all the ideas?

This modeling approach applies to assessment practices that deviate from parents' traditional conceptions of homework. Parents, for example, can self-assess their progress according to the outcomes you identify for the meeting or event. When parents experience success in a learning environment that differs from their previous time in school, they will be more likely to support you in all areas of your role as teacher, including your philosophy on homework.

Step 3: Provide strategies to parents.

Asking general questions that trigger learning for students is sometimes all a parent needs to do to help their kids who are working on an activity at home. Crafting possible responses to questions commonly asked by kids gives parents the language to keep the onus of learning on the student. Look at this boomerang model that throws the onus of thinking right back to the child:

BOOMERANG MODEL

What do I do if my child says, "I don't get this," when doing his/her homework?

Possible responses:

- How can you help yourself?

- What strategy can you use?

- Can you break the problem/question/prompt into smaller parts?

- Where should you start?

- What do you already know? How can you use that knowledge?

- Where is your confusion?

- Does your response make sense?

- What evidence do you have?

- Is this an explicit or inferred response?

These prompts are not content-specific and don't require parents to become the teacher. This way, parents can assume that homework will only be sent home when the teacher has reason to believe that the student can complete it independently. There should never be a need for the parent to provide instruction. Parent intervention creates students who lack perseverance, which is a valuable life and career skill. Spoon-feeding answers to students detracts from student growth.

Step 4: Share success stories.

Leverage the positive outcomes parents and students have had using the questions you've shared or the practices you've modeled. It will be powerful for parents to hear from their counterparts that these approaches work. As you share, "Mrs. Miller and Max had this conversation about last week's math unit…" Other parents may come up with more ideas and you will build a community of support within both your classroom and your students' homes.

Step 5: Add a "What to do if you're stuck" section to your classroom website.

For younger grades, it could be geared toward helping parents coach their students. For later grades, it could be targeted at students themselves, so they can practice self-sufficiency. Remember to inform parents to direct students toward the website for help, and resist the urge to guide them too much, which leads to learned helplessness. Your students can share model questions and responses on the site to support other students. As mentioned in Step 4, parents can also share their experiences and ideas. If you don't yet have a classroom website, this step is still actionable; try a Facebook group that serves as a conduit between you and your students' parents.

Step 6: Solicit feedback from parents, share it, and use it.

When you solicit parent feedback, you should share a summary of that feedback with the entire parent community, along with your plan for how you will use feedback to influence your future decisions. For example, if you ask parents for their thoughts on how effective the questioning techniques from Step 3 are, and 20 out of 25 parents love them, and five parents say they haven't had time to try them yet, you might look at the data and conclude that 80% is a pretty good approval rate. However, by sharing this information with all of the parents, you will notify those five parents that the majority of other parents are finding the questioning strategies valuable. Perhaps after the five parents view feedback from the others, you'll move closer to a 100% engagement rate. You can then follow-up with implementing ideas or suggestions that parents provided in the survey.

Step 7: Integrate parent professional development.

Consider which units provoke the most questions from students and/ or the most misconceptions about concepts or strategies. Design short courses to teach parents how to read assessment data, how to provide effective feedback, how to ask questions that push students to think for themselves, etc. Consider front-loading information when possible. For example, if the reproductive health unit is scheduled for April, invite parents to school in the winter months to preview the materials and think about how they will address student questions in light of the curriculum.

Consider the length of the message. If your PD topic can be summed up in under 10 minutes, just record a brief video and blast it out in a Remind link, on your website, Facebook, Twitter, and email blasts. Examples in this category might include: 3 Ways to Multiply, Best Tips for Getting Kids to Bed on Time, or How to Use TV Shows to Consider Author's Perspective. Always include applications parents and kids can transfer to home, ramping up the tools they have to support and extend learning after school hours.

Topics of greater complexity that would be more productive with interaction should be scheduled as face-to-face, then recorded and archived, and stored on your district's website for parents to view at their leisure. These topics might include: Understanding Students with ADHD or The Impact Reading at Home has on Student Learning. When planning these types of sessions, revisit the process you used in Steps 1 and 2 when reworking all kinds of parent meetings.

As the year progresses and you gather information from parents via Step 6, design sessions to tackle topics that parents have indicated are of interest. Take advantage of the opportunity to point out that parent modules are based on feedback collected from parents; this is the same process you use to plan engaging lessons and customizing for students. Demonstrate the power of personalized learning through this real-life example. Through these efforts to blend learning at home and school, you'll not only build allies with parents, but more important, students will have consistency in how learning opportunities are noticed and nourished at all times.

OVERCOMING PUSHBACK

Parents believe teaching is the educator's job, not theirs. Help parents understand that you believe in a partnership approach to learning. While it's the parents' responsibility to keep their children safe, they trust us to carry out that role during the school day. This is a reciprocal relationship, where our roles as educator/parent overlap. After all, parents really are their children's first and most influential teachers.

Parents are too busy to come to school to learn. Bring the learning to them. Create a podcast, make a video, or write an eBook. Leverage technology as much as you possibly can. If you work in a larger district, consider offering parents a range of times for face-to-face meetings; you can hold a meeting regarding upcoming field trips immediately after school one day, for example, and then repeat the same information after dinner time another night. If child care for the parents of younger students is an issue, solicit high school students to provide supervision for younger students while you're meeting with their parents. Find out what parents need and make it happen.

Parents often do the work for students. This pushback is one reason that traditional homework isn't effective. The solution is to stop assigning it. If you're not ready to let homework go completely, then arming parents with alternatives to spoon-feeding or taking over the assignment will keep the onus on students.

THE HACK IN ACTION

Crystal Morey has spent her career as a middle school math teacher. She is transitioning into a new role as a K-6 instructional coach, specializing in inquiry-based mathematics, in the Kent School District in Kent, Washington In this story, Crystal shares how she engages parents and helps to connect learning in the classroom to learning at home.

Crystal's Story

The transition to Common Core State Standards (CCSS) in mathematics has by no means been easy. Yet, as challenging as it has been for educators and students to understand and implement the new standards and practices, parents and families have little knowledge of what this change means and how it impacts their children. I have found that uncertainty often leads to numerous questions, which in turn can lead to frustrated parents.

To combat and even reverse these negative reactions, I have used several strategies to partner with families. These strategies have opened communication lines, mitigated tensions, and imparted vital information. As a result, we have created a relaxed learning atmosphere, adjusting the nature of student/family interactions so that students can work at home with the goal of learning, rather than the goal of getting all the answers right.

First, I no longer use open house night to go over classroom syllabi, etc. In lieu of traditional agenda items, I engage families in a hands-on problem-solving activity. I run a 10-minute mini lesson, much like I would with students, posing questions and asking parents to explain their answers to problems but refraining from labeling their answers correct or incorrect. In so doing, I model the types of exchanges that deepen learning. What is modeled shifts the role of parents to question students as opposed to correcting them, an action that often leads to conflict within the household and produces a hatred of mathematics.

Furthermore, mini lessons help me redefine the role that families play in Common Core mathematics. They are no longer expected to re-teach what I have already taught. Rather, I encourage them to listen and ask questions, without judgment. This strategy mimics the inquiry-based math lessons that are the focus of my classroom. Families learn the value of individual reflection over correctness. Most often, this discovery is a welcome relief to families, especially those who are unsure of their own capabilities in mathematics.

Second, if and when parents experience additional frustration as students struggle with new material, I engage the parents—along with their child—in hands-on learning. Instead of an intense parent meeting, I directly address the troubling standard in question, allowing both the parents and their children to further develop their understanding of the concept. These meetings employ a gradual release method.

First we define the standard. Second, I introduce the manipulatives that we use to help make sense of the mathematics. Third, I model a use of the manipulatives with a particular problem. Next, we (parents, student, and myself) all do a problem at the same time but individually, each sharing our mathematical models.

As we share, I myself use the question I encourage parents to use: "Can you explain your model so I can see what you see?" As each of us does so, I often see parents redefine and clarify their models. Finally, I present a new problem and ask if the student is willing to build a model. At that point, I take a step back and allow the families to ask this question, and whatever follow-up questions they may have, to their child directly.

At the end of the meeting, parents will understand the manipulatives used, and often, the challenges that the student is having. Thenceforth, parents are able to communicate more effectively with their kids about learning. I regularly receive thanks from parents for allowing them to experience "how math is taught these days." In improving their understanding of mathematical concepts and developing their questioning skills, parents strengthen their relationships with their kids, facilitating student progress in the classroom.

With increased trust in teachers and less uncertainty about mathematics, parents can calmly question their child rather than overwhelming him or her with lectures. Correspondingly, students aren't as stressed about performing perfectly. When families are more at ease, students become more creative and willing to take risks in their learning. Meanwhile, families become listeners, creating a laid-back atmosphere in which true learning occurs. These interactions with "new math" help parents see that the CCSS for math aim to create students who understand math concepts more deeply, rather than students who just walk through the steps of long division.

Third, I found that daily communication was incredibly important to conveying my expectations in terms of class work and homework. Using the app Remind, I took photos of all daily work, as well as explained any assignments that might be coming home. With nearly 75% of my families active on Remind, parents could instantly inform me when their student expressed frustration about the material and we were able to develop a plan before their household erupted into chaos over homework.

AUTHOR COMMENT

Remind sends messages straight to cell phones in the form of text messages. It's quick, direct, and doesn't require Internet access. Classroom- or school-sponsored Facebook pages are also a successful means of reaching parents, many of whom use Facebook daily.

True, these three measures take up some of my "out of the classroom" time. However, when I address a problem in a proactive manner and make myself available for communication, families begin to trust in the educational system, meaning that they become partners and we all get on the same team.

When we treat parents as partners in education, they become part of the team. There isn't a parent out there who doesn't want his/her child to succeed. If we provide parents with tools for facilitating student success, honoring their key roles as co-educators in their children's lives, we—the teachers and the parents—convey a consistent and powerful message to students.

Explicit examples, experiences, and concrete tools are all ways to help parents broaden their perspectives on how their kids learn. With a newfound conception of issues like homework, parents can let go of outdated strategies that might have worked for students of a previous century but don't meet the needs of kids today.

HACK 10

DISPLAY GROWTH

Empower students to track their improvement and display progress

"Not everything that counts can be counted, and not everything that can be counted counts."
—ALBERT EINSTEIN

THE PROBLEM: HOMEWORK GRADES ARE MEANINGLESS

L EARNING HAS NO meaningful impact beyond what students take away and can apply. When teachers attempt to label what they think students know, they erode the learning process by taking the importance of growth away, minimizing it into a complete/not complete category. Along with mandatory nightly homework assignments, many schools require that homework be graded, assuming that grades are what motivate students to do the work and that grades communicate what students learned. How many times have you heard a student ask if homework will be graded, as if the answer will determine how much effort will be expended? This challenge of student commitment to a grade coupled with the practice of quantifying student learning undermines students' intrinsic motivation.

If we want to make learning student-driven and meaningful, we need to avoid practices that undermine that effort because:

- Assessment of homework is often arbitrary and non-specific. Teachers track whether or not work is complete, issuing check minuses, checks, or check pluses, but do not evaluate students' mastery of the material.

- Students often receive little to no feedback for their homework, as there is just too much of it for teachers to make meaningful comments.

- Students might learn skills the wrong way if no feedback is given. The traditional approach to homework creates challenges down the road, as students aren't even aware that they are doing things incorrectly.

- Students take little to no ownership of their work, often copying friends' assignments. They therefore have no idea what they know and can do, which is problematic when it comes time to use those skills in other learning experiences.

THE HACK: DISPLAY GROWTH

Since there is no proven "right way" to assess and track student learning, the most effective option is to turn this responsibility over to the students. Because learning should stem from intrinsic motivation, teachers can spend time showing students how to track the feedback and their progress from long-term learning experiences. This way students will learn to reflect on their growth, set better goals, and be accountable for their own growth.

As we stop forcing kids to comply with policies that don't facilitate learning and start making out-of-class work meaningful, we need to help students develop an understanding of who they are as learners, so they are able to express what they know and can do. Students can then use time outside of class in ways that best support their individual learning needs.

WHAT YOU CAN DO TOMORROW

- **Stop collecting and grading every assignment.** For homework that is assigned (on a more flexible basis), don't collect or grade it. Be judicious in what you are assigning; give feedback where appropriate in class when using the connected projects with lessons being taught, and ask kids to keep everything in a safe and organized place. If students are doing work electronically, they can easily store their documents on Google Drive and organize them appropriately there in folders.

- **Enrich student growth with only purposeful assignments.** When students ask if the homework will be graded, make sure to say that it doesn't matter. All work that is happening in the classroom has a purpose; each assignment is intended to fulfill an objective, enriching student growth and learning in the process. Make sure students understand that you wouldn't ask them to do something that isn't worth their time. Be transparent in how work connects to what's going on in the classroom, and why it matters. Don't be afraid to let students voice their opinions. Truly listen to them, as this will help with buy-in moving forward.

- **Track student progress independently.** Students will need to have a space where they track their learning. Help them create this space by holding a class brainstorming session about different ways to maintain the information. Some students will prefer to write it down, so they should use the back of their notebooks and set up a page with three or four columns to prepare for tracking their work. More techy students might prefer to use a Google Doc, with a table or spreadsheet. Make sure to get access to these digital spaces and regularly check in with students who use notebooks as well.

Date and assignment	Feedback provided	Strategy to be employed	Reflection/action plan or goals

Figure 10.1

A BLUEPRINT FOR FULL IMPLEMENTATION

Step 1: Illuminate success criteria.

In order for students to truly be responsible for their progress, they will need to know what success looks like, and what it takes to achieve mastery in a particular skill or of a particular subject. Designate class time for reviewing learning standards and sharing exemplars that illustrate your expectations. It's a good idea to refrain from giving students a sample of the actual work they will be doing, as they might copy it, but you can certainly offer models from a different content area or lesson that demonstrate mastery just as effectively.

Instruct students to review the models and as a class, make sure you debrief and annotate. At that point, students can develop a checklist of expectations. Take time to do this exercise whenever you are teaching new skills or content. If you are using rubrics, make sure to design the rubrics with the students based on overall outcomes and objectives. This may occur through a class brainstorm or in small groups, depending on the size of your class. More specifics on how to involve students in developing success criteria can be found in Hack 7 of Starr's *Hacking Assessment.*

In order for students to track their progress independently at home, students must first know what they are looking for in class.

Step 2: Track progress on concepts and ideas.

Once students have a solid foundational understanding of learning standards and expectations, they have a clear idea of what they need to be tracking. As you're working through new ideas, always make it a point to ensure that students know what mastery looks like. Then show them how to fill out a chart like Figure 10.1 that lays out information in a clear and organized way. Encourage students to go back to this chart not just when they are adding new feedback and strategies, but also to reflect on their progress once they have mastered the skill in question. Consider the example in Figure 10.2.

Date and assignment	Feedback provided	Strategy to be employed	Reflection/action plan or goals
9/30 Poetry analysis draft	Thesis needs to focus more closely on an author's craft	Peer review, re-review the poem to address what the best device for the paper is	Thesis was revised to address the tone and diction of poem and evidence was written down to support thesis. Asked a peer to read and review new thesis for clarity. In the future, will make sure to clearly write what is being proven.
	Context needs to be developed to engage the reader	Consider larger general connections by brainstorming ideas	Wrote 3 sentences about choices, the larger more general theme of the poem to engage the reader. In the future, I will remember to consider how I use context to tie the essay together.

Figure 10.2

Step 3: Reflect as a part of the learning process.

There is nothing more powerful than reflection in the learning process. Students are able to look back, consider their progress, and gauge their own levels of understanding. Since teachers can only see so much on the page or through a project, we must teach students to share what they know in a way that offers us deeper insight into whether they have mastered the material. In using reflection as a tool in class, students learn to evaluate their tracked progress, discuss their goals and describe how they were able to meet or exceed standards, with specific reference to the strategies employed. Connections become more transparent and students can see the way their progress develops over a longer period of time.

Reflection doesn't need to be written. If students are more inclined to employ audio, face-to-face conferences, or video, these methods are appropriate so long as the focus remains on student work and growth.

Step 4: Incorporate goal setting into the process.

In addition to understanding success criteria, students should control the direction in which they want their learning to go. Since students move at different paces and need different kinds of help, it makes sense to let them set their own individualized goals, in alignment with class objectives. Teachers are then able to give more targeted feedback based on the student's particular aims and timeframe.

Classes can celebrate the achievement of goals by posting student progress updates on a wall display for both students and teachers to reference. These displays publicly recognize student growth, demystifying the formative part of the process and embracing the messy learning in between. Henceforth, by making student goals public, wall postings hold students accountable to the goals they have set for themselves.

Step 5: Confer with students regularly.

In addition to reflection and goal setting, the feedback you provide students and the feedback they provide each other lies at the heart of learning. Students need to receive targeted, personalized feedback that lets them know they are moving in the right direction and identifies areas in which they must continue to grow. Teachers can provide feedback in many different ways. Depending on the size and style of your classroom, you'll need to decide what works best. Methods a teacher can use include: writing on the document or project; voice feedback on an app like Voxer or through a Chrome extension on Google Docs; and face-to-face feedback in a small group, or one-on-one where needed. Students should be given feedback in a timely fashion, so that they can quickly adjust their approaches, and poor habits or misinformation do not sink in.

If there is a disparity in student-teacher feedback, it is essential to escalate the conversation. Make sure to have a one-to-one conference with the student whose work is being discussed and begin a dialogue to better clarify what is meant. This ongoing conversation will ensure any miscommunication or fundamentally conflicting feedback gets resolved in a meaningful and useful way.

Students value the time we share with them and the more individual attention we give them, the better. This can happen in class, after class, or through technology. Short check-ins allow students to ask clarifying questions, obtain affirmation of their knowledge, and express any concerns they may have. These check-ins should be student-led, with the teacher present as a sounding board.

Step 6: Eliminate the "Justice Mindset."

Always make sure to check your judgment at the door and try not to let the "justice mindset" cloud the way you help students. Many of us were raised in settings where compliance was valued and therefore we need to refocus what we focus on in the learning process. The justice mindset is the idea that kids should be penalized when they don't do what we want instead of looking at learning first. Progress isn't about short-term points and compliance; it's about mastery and achievement over time. We need to keep reiterating this philosophy to students, teachers, and parents, reminding them that students are in charge of their own learning and that homework doesn't need to be mandatory or graded in order to be valuable.

OVERCOMING PUSHBACK

Many folks will say that kids can't be responsible for tracking their own growth and that they won't even complete homework that isn't being assessed. But just because homework isn't assigned every day and/or isn't being collected doesn't mean students aren't putting in the effort. To the contrary, students are setting learning objectives that fit their individual needs and are getting something even more valuable by tracking their own progress.

Homework needs to be collected for kids to take it seriously.
Although we often think we must hold kids accountable and/or
penalize them to incentivize homework, students take their learning
seriously when we teach them to undertake their own assessments.
Furthermore, if the work itself is something that students had a part in
creating, they don't mind completing it, particularly if they can do so at
their own pace. The more involved students are in the homework process, the more seriously they treat the work, with or without a grade.

**Homework needs to be graded for students to complete it with
pride.** Students may indeed be trained to wait for a grade to judge
how well they did the work. Ultimately, however, this type of compliance has less to do with learning and more to do with playing school.
In relying heavily on grading, the system places too much power in
the teacher's hands and not enough responsibility in the student's.
Teachers and schools need to support learning in a way that validates
the process more than the grade so students take pride in the progress rather than just the final product.

There should be consequences when students fail to comply. There
is little evidence to suggest that forcing students to do their work will
produce better learning or higher achievement. When work outside
the classroom isn't meaningful to students, they don't feel compelled
to do it, so the teacher must find other ways to get students to connect
with learning. Teachers must share why the work is useful and relevant to students' lives rather than threaten detention, lowered grades,
or a suspension of involvement in extracurricular activities or sports.

Students aren't capable of tracking their own learning. Students
are more capable than we give them credit for. When expectations
are raised, they often surprise us with their ability to act maturely
and exceed these expectations. If given the right tools, class time

to practice, and specific, timely feedback, students can successfully track their own learning. In many cases, students know their needs and goals better than anyone and find a method that works for them as long as there are protocols in place that call for these tracking processes and behaviors. Those students who require more support can get it in the form of one-on-one appointments with teachers or from peer buddies who help scaffold the process.

Tracking learning is the teacher's job, not the student's. A teacher has many responsibilities when working with children of all ages, but the most important one is getting kids to take ownership of and accountability for their learning. This is not something you can expect to magically happen. Rather, teachers must provide support, transparency, and feedback, working with students until they are ready to take control. Teachers must monitor student progress, offering guidance along the way without doing the work for them. When a teacher decides that a student can't track learning on his or her own, the student will believe it to be so, and may grow apathetic.

Some students will take longer than others to learn how to handle this responsibility, but we can't give up on any of them. Ultimately, however, tracking progress and growing through reflection will be integral to each child's learning experience. Once students can effectively do these things, the teacher has succeeded in preparing them for college and/or a career.

THE HACK IN ACTION

A hallmark of Starr's AP Literature and Composition classroom is student reflection and self-assessment. In this story, you'll see how Starr empowers students to track their own progress at home, making the learning process fluid from home to school.

Starr's Story

Each year I embark on a journey to help students become self-starting learners. Imagine having a room full of students who know how to review their own work, find areas of strength and challenges, and ask for strategies to improve going forward. With our in-class process, students set goals, reflect, receive feedback from me and/or their peers, and then continue to revise, often by choice at home, until they are proud of the work they have done.

One student, Alicia Massey, did a great job of tracking my feedback on her assignments throughout the year. When it was convenient for her, usually late at night, she would insert the date and the assignment into a Google Doc, then cut and paste the comments I had placed along the side of her original document. Tracking each piece of feedback dutifully, she'd often come in for extra help, asking me if she didn't understand what I had written or if she wanted guidance on strategies for improvement. Other students tracked their feedback in their notebooks in similar ways, asking questions of their peers when workshop time was given in class. Usually, more than one student would experience the difficulty that Alicia expressed, which I could then address in class with mini lessons if students didn't get it on their own after working with peers. This shared confusion indicated that perhaps I didn't teach the concept well enough or that maybe I should try teaching it a different way.

AUTHOR COMMENT

Teaching students to use feedback and self-reflect can begin in elementary school. Encouraging students to use time at home to re-read their writing and flag areas in which they would like feedback is an effective way to introduce this type of system. Self-reflection can then be done at home as a part of review of content and future goal setting.

This feedback cycle allowed Alicia and other students to regularly revisit challenges they faced, making additional attempts to improve in these areas. Drawing upon the feedback and strategies provided, the students could apply their learning to the new task and then reflect on their growth at the end of the process.

One thing Alicia did particularly well was to use this reflection time to show where and how she was able to apply the learning from the feedback she had tracked, and articulate how the process of tracking had improved her writing: *"After creating my intro-duction paragraph, I went through the book and selected evidence that I might want to use in the paper. I typed out and listed direct quotes, citing them as shown in class. I didn't use every quote that I typed up. I narrowed it down only to the ones that applied to the statements I was saying. Using another piece of feedback provided in the poetry analysis essay—'make sure that it clearly ties back to your thesis'—I tried really hard to make sure I was bringing up points that correlated back to my thesis."*

Because systems were set up in class to make it easy for students to know what was expected outside the classroom, Alicia was able to meet learning standards in a meaningful way and grow her level of mastery.

Alicia describes in a reflection how she applied this feedback to her new work. As students become more aware of their areas of strength and challenge and accountable for what they know and can do, they are better equipped to learn moving forward. Figure 10.3 is an excerpt from the feedback log that Alicia kept throughout the year.

Poetry Analysis Paper 10/18

- ○ Your introductory paragraph must include your thesis section. Your second paragraph has your thesis, but it also goes into analysis already. I'd like you to combine the context with the thesis before going into the analysis
- ○ What is the impact of the rhyme on the reader? Make sure that it clearly ties back to your thesis.
- ○ You need a transition between these two ideas rather than just jumping to the next rhyme.
- ○ How does this inquisitive tone support the theme of grief and rhyme scheme? Don't throw everything in there – only use information/evidence that supports what you are trying to prove.
- ○ Avoid the second person in academic writing
- ○ Yes...thanks for telling me what the rhyme does. How does it do that?
- ○ Make sure there is a transition here to develop this idea without just repeating ideas.
- ○ There seems to be a gap here...what the cohesion – how do these ideas go together?
- ○ Make sure to state with authority.
- ○ Avoid saying "I believe" or inserting the first person.
- ○ The concluding paragraph just summarizes. We need to move beyond restating and actually leave the reader thinking about the topic or context.

Figure 10.3

As we begin to make accountability an expectation in our classes, students have the opportunity to work at their own pace, doing only what they need to in order to accomplish their goals. Feedback coupled with teacher- and peer-provided strategies and reflection facilitates student ownership. The skills developed through this process will translate to students' adult lives.

When we empower students to take control of their learning, magic happens—and not just the kind that is learned at Hogwarts. Students become more articulate about what they know and can do and spend time really advocating for their own growth. These skills are far more essential in today's world than compliance and following directions. Students gain a voice in their process and are equipped and unafraid to ask for the support they need.

As we continue to reimagine what homework can be, we need to remember what the point of education is: to help students become more independent and engaged in their own learning by shifting toward a more student-centered experience. The less we make out-of-class activities about grades and compliance, the more meaningful they will be over time, empowering students to grow and develop ownership of what they know.

CONCLUSION

It's time to rethink how learning happens outside of school

THE HOMEWORK CONVERSATION is often one of great debate, eliciting passion on both sides of the argument. We're not interested in getting into a spitting contest about whether or not homework should be given at all. Rather, we're questioning the long-standing notion that homework will be used as busywork without an intentional purpose beyond the hope of building good study habits. So much of education is being reconsidered; it's time that homework goes through the same serious consideration as every other curriculum, instruction, and assessment decision we make as professionals.

Just because homework has always looked a certain way doesn't mean *that* way is the best for the students we work with or the families they go home to. Worksheets, reading logs, spelling lists, and hours of math problems aren't great academic interventions, which is why we must re-evaluate what we are asking students and families to do after the school day ends. Every time we deviate from tradition, we take a risk and try something new, hoping that it may be more appropriate for the students we serve today. Each of these leaps comes with potential pushback and failure, but we will never find the necessary tools to propel students forward if we continue to do things the way we always have. Mistakes happen; Einstein knew this. In fact, he and others like him believed that mistakes were necessary for growth.

Student learning is complex and impossible to simplify into a flow chart of "do this, then do that." Factors such as level of student interest, rapport with the teacher, and relevance play a much larger role in accessing learning than we might think. We encourage you to buck the systems that make assumptions about homework and that don't engage in the dialogue revealing the pros and cons of seven hours of school and additional work at home on top of that.

Filling students' time with oodles of work beyond the school day sends a negative message about how we value what students do outside of school. Since kids are often overscheduled with other kinds of learning, like music lessons, dance, sports or clubs, adding more schoolwork only complicates matters further. In these other activities, students are often practicing what they learn and/or developing skills that can make them more tenacious in their approach to learning.

Whether practicing an instrument or dance routine, students are building chops, increasing stamina, and learning from their mistakes. Each time a goal isn't scored or a pass incomplete, it is an opportunity for students to see that all learning takes time. Kids need the right opportunities to make mistakes, try again, learn, and improve; this is how we grow. Ironically, this process may be evident with their sports teams or piano lessons, but it may be disconnected somehow from their learning in school. The more time we allow kids to associate this process with learning, whether in or out of school, the more perseverance they develop for working out problems they'll face later in life. Plus, downtime can really work wonders for stress and anxiety, which kids need. They need to run off their energy and play, even if they aren't on a team. A family walk or a bike ride present great opportunities to observe and communicate about a variety of important wonderings.

So, as we invite families and schools on this journey of changing traditional homework, we communicate regularly about what we learn when risks are taken and we collaborate to improve the learning atmosphere for all involved. These useful reflections will continue to build capacity in our students and their relationships with peers, teachers, family members, and their understanding of the world.

The world is a vast and inspiring place where learning is constantly happening, usually when we don't even realize it. We need to harness the power of everyday life to connect the lessons of the classroom to students' existence outside of school. In this way, learning becomes more meaningful, and its purpose more transparent. Accountability and responsibility can be taught without nightly homework, and the lessons learned at home when we make families partners can profoundly impact the classroom as well. Think about how sharing these experiences can help other children make more concrete connections, especially if they aren't already using family time in this way.

We started our book with Einstein's quote, *"Anyone who has never made a mistake has never tried anything new."* Reflect on his words. They give you permission and even challenge you to rethink your current practice, to try something new, and to inspire learning outside your classroom.

OTHER BOOKS IN THE
HACK LEARNING SERIES

HACKING EDUCATION
10 Quick Fixes For Every School

By Mark Barnes (@markbarnes19) & Jennifer Gonzalez (@cultofpedagogy)

In the bestselling *Hacking Education*, Mark Barnes and Jennifer Gonzalez employ decades of teaching experience and hundreds of discussions with education thought leaders to show you how to find and hone the quick fixes that every school and classroom need. Using a Hacker's mentality, they provide one Aha moment after another with 10 Quick Fixes For Every School—solutions to everyday problems and teaching methods that any teacher or administrator can implement immediately.

"Barnes and Gonzalez don't just solve problems; they turn teachers into hackers—a transformation that is right on time."

— Don Wettrick, author of Pure Genius

MAKE WRITING
5 Teaching Strategies That Turn Writers
Workshop Into a Maker Space

By Angela Stockman (@angelastockman)

Everyone's favorite education blogger and writing coach, Angela Stockman, turns teaching strategies and practices upside down in the bestselling, *Make Writing*. She spills you out of your chair, shreds your lined paper, and launches you and your writer's workshop into the maker space! Stockman provides five right-now writing strategies that reinvent instruction and inspire both young and adult writers to express ideas with tools that have rarely, if ever, been considered. Make Writing is a fast-paced journey inside Stockman's Western New York Young Writer's Studio, alongside the students there who learn how to write and how to make, employing Stockman's unique teaching methods.

"Offering suggestions for using new materials in old ways, thoughtful questions, and specific tips for tinkering and finding new audiences, this refreshing book is inspiring and practical in equal measure."

—AMY LUDWIG VANDERWATER, AUTHOR AND

TEACHER

HACKING ASSESSMENT
10 Ways to Go Gradeless in a Traditional Grades School

By Starr Sackstein (@mssackstein)

In the bestselling *Hacking Assessment,* award-winning teacher and world-renowned formative assessment expert Starr Sackstein unravels one of education's oldest mysteries: How to assess learning without grades—even in a school that uses numbers, letters, GPAs, and report cards. While many educators can only muse about the possibility of a world without grades, teachers like Sackstein are reimagining education. In this unique, eagerly-anticipated book, Sackstein shows you exactly how to create a remarkable no-grades classroom like hers, a vibrant place where students grow, share, thrive, and become independent learners who never ask, "What's this worth?"

"The beauty of the book is that it is not an empty argument against grades—but rather filled with valuable alternatives that are practical and will help to refocus the classroom on what matters most."

— ADAM BELLOW, WHITE HOUSE PRESIDENTIAL INNOVATION FELLOW

HACKING THE COMMON CORE
10 Strategies for Amazing Learning in a Standardized World

By Michael Fisher (@fisher1000)

In *Hacking the Common Core,* longtime teacher and CCSS specialist Mike Fisher shows you how to bring fun back to learning, with 10 amazing hacks for teaching all Core subjects, while engaging students and making learning fun. Fisher's experience and insights help teachers and parents better understand close reading, balancing fiction and nonfiction, using projects with the Core and much more. *Hacking the Common Core* provides read-tonight-implement-tomorrow strategies for teaching the standards in fun and engaging ways, improving teaching and learning for students, parents, and educators.

HACKING LEADERSHIP
10 Ways Great Leaders Inspire Learning That Teachers, Students, and Parents Love

By Joe Sanfelippo (@joesanfelippoFC) and Tony Sinanis (@tonysinanis)

In the runaway bestseller *Hacking Leadership,* renowned school leaders Joe Sanfelippo and Tony Sinanis bring readers inside schools that few stakeholders have ever seen—places where students not only come first but have a unique voice in teaching and learning. Sanfelippo and Sinanis ignore the bureaucracy that stifles many leaders, focusing instead on building a culture of engagement, transparency, and most important, fun. *Hacking Leadership* has superintendents, principals, and teacher leaders around the world employing strategies they never before believed possible.

"The authors do a beautiful job of helping leaders focus inward, instead of outward. This is an essential read for leaders who are, or want to lead, learner-centered schools."

—GEORGE COUROS, AUTHOR OF *THE INNOVATOR'S MINDSET*

HACKING LITERACY
5 Ways To Turn Any Classroom Into a Culture Of Readers

By Gerard Dawson (@gerarddawson3)

In *Hacking Literacy*, classroom teacher, author, and reading consultant Gerard Dawson reveals 5 simple ways any educator or parent can turn even the most reluctant reader into a thriving, enthusiastic lover of books. Dawson cuts through outdated pedagogy and standardization, turning reading theory into practice, sharing powerful reading strategies, and providing what *Hack Learning Series* readers have come to expect—actionable, do-it-tomorrow strategies that can be built into long-term solutions.

HACKING ENGAGEMENT
50 Tips & Tools to Engage Teachers and Learners Daily

By James Alan Sturtevant (@jamessturtevant)

Some students hate your class. Others are just bored. Many are too nice, or too afraid, to say anything about it. Don't let it bother you; it happens to the best of us. But now, it's **time to engage!** In *Hacking Engagement*, the seventh book in the *Hack Learning Series*, veteran high school teacher, author, and popular podcaster James Sturtevant provides 50—that's right—five-oh-tips and tools that will engage even the most reluctant learners daily.

HACK LEARNING RESOURCES

All Things Hack Learning:

hacklearning.org

The Entire Hack Learning Series on Amazon:

hacklearningbooks.com

Blend Education:

Hack Learning's Digital Content Partner:

blendeducation.org

The Hack Learning Podcast, hosted by Mark Barnes:

hacklearningpodcast.com

Hack Learning on Twitter:

@HackMyLearning

#HackLearning

#HackingEngagement

#HackingHomework

#HackingLeadership

#HackingLiteracy

#HackingPBL

#MakeWriting

The Hack Learning Academy:

hacklearningacademy.com

Hack Learning on Facebook:

facebook.com/hacklearningseries

The Hack Learning Store:

hacklearningstore.com

ABOUT THE AUTHORS

Starr Sackstein is a teacher/coach at Long Island City High School in Queens, New York, and a two-time Bammy Awards Finalist. She is an ASCD Emerging Leader and a popular speaker. Starr is the author of *Hacking Assessment, Teaching Mythology Exposed, Blogging for Educators, Teaching Students to Self Assess, The Power of Questioning*, and *Empower Students to Give Feedback*. She blogs on Education Week Teacher at "Work in Progress" and co-moderates the popular #sunchat on Twitter. Starr's 2016 TEDx Talk chronicles her journey to creating a no-grades classroom. Balancing a busy career of writing and teaching with being the mom to 10-year-old Logan is a challenging adventure. Seeing the world through his eyes reminds her why education needs to change for every child.

Talk to Starr Sackstein
mssackstein@gmail.com
@MsSackstein on Twitter
Starr Sackstein, MJE Facebook Fan page

Connie Hamilton, Ed.S., is the curriculum director in Saranac Community Schools in Michigan. As a professional development expert and educational consultant, she uses her masterful questioning techniques to help schools focus on systems to support student achievement. On Twitter, Connie has grown her professional learning network through her thoughtful tweets and connections she's made as founder and moderator of #TMchat. Being an educator and the mother of three teenagers, Connie approaches homework from both a classroom and kitchen-table perspective. Seeing the downside of poorly coordinated and planned homework assignments in her own home inspired her to write *Hacking Homework*.

Talk to Connie Hamilton, Ed.S.
www.conniehamilton.org
conniehamilton12@gmail.com
@conniehamilton on Twitter

ACKNOWLEDGEMENTS

WE WANTED TO thank everyone who helped make this book possible. Aside from being a really amazing collaborative experience, we've learned so much from each person's contributions.

First, thanks to Mark Barnes for always being available to help out with ideas and follow our crazy whims.

A big thank you to Justin Birckbichler, Peter Cameron, Cathy Cooper, Tamra Dollar, Sean Gaillard, Bethany Hill, Crystal Morey, Jennifer Scheffer and Don Wettrick, who answered the bat signal almost immediately and shared their learning with us to help make this project as special as it is.

A special thanks to the students who answered our survey and shared their honest opinions about their experiences with homework. Since this book is really about making learning better for you, your words and wisdom are what matter most.

PUBLICATIONS

Times 10 is helping all education stakeholders improve every aspect of teaching and learning. We are committed to solving big problems with simple ideas. We bring you content from experts, shared through multiple channels, including books, podcasts, and an array of social networks. Our mantra is simple: Read it today; fix it tomorrow.

Stay in touch with us at #HackLearning on Twitter and on the Hack Learning Facebook page. To work with our authors and consultants, visit our Team page at hacklearning.org.

Index

12th man, 156, 169, 172
3 and out, 126, 150-151, 173, 192, 197, 199, 207-208, 212, 214, 216
49ers, see San Francisco 49ers
4th down, 5, 10, 60, 69-71, 126, 174, 211, 270, 298

A
Advanced NFL statistics, 71
AFC championship, 76, 96, 136, 144, 156, 212, 228, 244, 283, 298
AFL-NFL merger, 16
Aggregate career statistics, 64
Amendola, 196, 211, 214-215, 228-229, 247, 251-252, 255, 270, 295, 299, 301-303
American Conference, 73, 95, 135
American Football Conference, 18, 204
American Professional, 13
Analytical Tools, 89, 91, 93
ANOVA, 51
Arbitrage, 6, 10-11, 74, 83, 89-91, 124-131, 133, 135, 141, 173, 176, 180, 189, 201, 209, 216, 280, 288, 294, 298, 300
  Pure arbitrage, 90
Arizona Cardinals, 13, 31, 105, 107, 116, 156, 181-182, 187, 189-190, 194, 204, 217, 224, 226-227, 229, 232, 240, 249, 269, 273-274, 278-279, 282, 285, 307, 322, 334, 337
Atlanta Falcons, 6, 28, 32-33, 42, 74, 83, 91, 101, 103, 105, 107, 116-118, 121, 128-129, 132, 136-139, 142-147, 149, 183, 185, 204, 232-234, 237,

239-241, 243-246, 248-253, 257, 266-268, 272-274, 278-279, 282, 285, 289, 294, 297, 327, 330, 334
Autocorrelation, 85
Availability, 92, 203
Average position salary, 48-49, 55

B
Baltimore Ravens, 14-15, 18, 21, 29, 31-32, 71, 101, 103, 105, 107-108, 111-112, 118, 123-124, 129, 133, 137, 139-140, 143-144, 147-153, 155, 159, 163, 180, 182, 186-187, 190, 194-197, 199, 202, 204, 211, 234, 273-274, 278-279, 282-284, 334
Bears, see Chicago Bears
Beastmode, 270, 277-278
Behavioral finance analysis, 193
Benching, 104, 274
Benchmark, 68, 84, 307
Bengals, see Cincinnati Bengals
Benoit, A. 36, 38, 257
Best teams.
  defensive, 172
  offensive teams, 172
Betfair, 6, 69, 85, 90, 92, 96, 102, 108-109, 111-112, 115, 124, 130-132, 135, 139-140, 142-143, 150, 159, 166-168, 171-172, 175-176, 180, 182, 185-186, 189-190, 194-195, 207, 210, 212-213, 218-220, 225, 230, 242, 296
Beuoy, Mike 179
Bid-ask prices, 158
Bid-ask spreads, 89, 115, 201
Bills, see Buffalo Bills

Billy Ball, 73
Binary wager, 63, 310
Blount, LeGarrette 24, 52-53, 76, 169,
    211-212, 214, 216, 220, 226, 232,
    243, 247, 249, 252, 272, 294, 300-
    303, 324
Bookmaker, 63-64, 93
Boza, Joey 267
Bradley-Taylor model, 61-62
Bradshaw, 20, 123, 126-127, 216, 236
Brady, Tom, 6, 30-31, 36, 38, 52, 68-
    71, 73, 76-77, 80, 83, 104, 117, 123-
    127, 133, 137, 140, 143, 148-150,
    153, 155-156, 167, 169-170, 179-180,
    182, 195-197, 208, 210-212, 214-216,
    218, 221, 226, 228-232, 235-236, 240,
    242, 244, 246-255, 266-268, 270-271,
    276, 280-282, 284, 294-295, 298-299,
    301-303, 321-322, 326, 335
Brees, Drew 39, 80, 86, 98, 117, 123,
    131, 153, 156, 158, 166, 176, 231,
    235, 268, 271, 285, 296, 321-322,
    336-337
Broncos, see Denver Broncos
Browns, see Cleveland Browns
Buccaneers, see Tampa Bay Buccaneers
Buffalo Bills, 16, 19, 25-26, 28, 105,
    107, 116, 173, 180, 183, 185, 204,
    229, 231, 273-274, 277-279, 282-284,
    297, 334
Bunker, 176, 242

C
Cardinals, see Arizona Cardinals
Carolina Panthers, 31, 32, 42, 105, 107,
    116, 158-160, 163-164, 167, 183, 187,
    189-191, 193-194, 196-199, 204, 208,
    217, 220-221, 224, 227, 229-231, 268,
    272-274, 277-279, 282, 297, 307, 322,
    327, 330, 334
Carr, Derek 153, 232-233, 235-237, 249,
    266, 286
Chamberlain, 35
Championship game, 13-14, 16, 28, 31,
    96, 136, 193, 200, 228, 277, 298
Chargers, see LA Chargers

Chess rating system, 79
Chicago Bears, 13, 18, 20, 22, 24, 26-
    27, 30-31, 101, 103, 105, 107-108,
    116, 166, 172, 202, 204, 271-274,
    278-279, 282, 324, 330, 334
Chiefs, see Kansas City Chiefs
Cincinnati Bengals, 24, 26, 105, 107,
    118, 121, 129, 137, 165-166, 182-
    183, 186-187, 190-191, 204, 194, 217-
    218, 223-224, 269, 273-274, 278-279,
    282-284, 324
Cleveland Browns, 14-16, 18, 29, 42,
    105, 107-108, 116, 183, 185, 204,
    250, 268, 271, 273-274, 278-279, 281-
    282, 307, 324, 328, 334
Clowney, Jadeveon, 39, 242, 285
Coach of the year, 190, 249, 322
Coaches, 5, 9, 25, 35-37, 70-71, 76-77,
    149, 156, 220, 243, 248, 251, 281,
    306, 309, 321-322, 324
Coast offense, 23
Coin toss, 81, 98-99, 125, 210, 214,
    227-228, 298
Cole, Jason 108, 122
Colts, see Indianapolis Colts
Comeback player of the year, 166, 195
Commission, 64, 96, 108, 136, 153, 171,
    194
Conference Championship, 88, 96, 100,
    118, 136, 169, 193, 203, 298, 330
Consistency, 67-68
Conversion, 22, 25, 70-72, 77, 126, 131,
    143, 152, 170, 175, 200, 209, 230,
    251-252, 281, 310
    two point conversion, 25, 70, 77,
    131, 143, 152
Cowboys, see Dallas Cowboys
Crowd noise, 79

D
Dallas Cowboys, 21, 25-29, 35, 42, 85,
    105, 107, 112, 116-117, 158, 175,
    183, 185, 187, 191-195, 199-200, 204,
    232-234, 237, 238, 240-241, 245-246,
    249, 272-275, 278-279, 281-282, 284-
    286, 326, 328, 334, 337

Davis, Nate 334

Decisions, 36, 48, 70, 76-77, 92, 228-229, 251

Defensive player of the year, 195, 218, 233, 236, 242, 249, 299

Denver Broncos, 16, 21, 24, 26, 28-29, 32, 74, 84, 92, 105, 107-108, 116-118, 123-124, 128-129, 132-133, 136-140, 143-144, 155-156, 158-160, 164, 167-177, 182, 185-187, 191, 193. 194, 200-202, 204, 217, 220, 224, 227-231, 234, 237, 267-270, 273-274, 276-279, 289, 282, 284, 289, 307, 324, 330, 334, 335, 337

Detroit Lions, 15-16, 18, 28-29, 42, 84, 105, 107, 116-118, 128-129, 160, 182, 187, 190-192, 194, 200, 218, 232-234, 237-240, 244, 271, 273-274, 278-279, 282, 286, 322, 324, 330, 334

Difference rating
  away, 81, 99
  home, 81

Divisional Playoffs, 19, 96, 118, 136, 167, 193, 225, 294

Dolphins, see Miami Dolphins

Dominance, 35, 267, 334

Dr Z's bets, 69

Dynasty potential dashed, 328

E

Eagles, see Philadelphia Eagles

Efficient markets, 11, 89

Elias Sports, 86

Elite quarterbacks, 123-124, 127

Elo ratings, 10-11, 79, 81-88, 97, 99-103, 105-112, 114, 116-117, 120-121, 124-125, 127-128, 130, 132, 158, 165, 179-182, 184-185, 187, 189-191, 194, 197, 199-200, 205, 207, 210, 212, 214, 234, 258, 270-272, 279-280, 282-283, 289, 292, 294-296, 299, 305-320, 538

  Elo Evolution, 105-106, 127, 289

  Evaluating, 87

  Playoff odds, 184, 205

  Swetye Elo ratings, 81, 97, 101, 292

  Testing the Elo, 310

  Elo vs Vegas vs Reality, 185

Elway, John 27, 92, 123, 140, 202, 217, 229, 267

ESPN, 83, 273-274, 279, 282, 322, 335, 337

Expected Value of Field Position, 59-60

F

Falcons, see Arizona Falcons

False starts, 156

Favorite-longshot bias, 6, 10, 89, 92-94, 98, 109, 257

Foxborough, 133, 143, 194, 218, 267

Framing, 92

Free agents, 324-325

Fumble recovery, 125

Fumbles, 67, 132, 161, 165, 169, 173-174, 189, 193, 200, 230, 238-239, 253-254, 267, 274-275, 278

G

Game for the ages, 6, 130, 165, 213, 245, 296

General investment ideas, 135

Giants, see New York Giants

Give-aways, 161

Goff, Jared, 268, 275-276

Green Bay Packers, 13-14, 16-19, 28, 32, 35, 83, 91, 101-103, 105, 107, 109, 116-118, 123-124, 128-129, 132, 136-138, 141, 158, 164, 166-167, 180, 182, 185-187, 190-191, 193-194, 199-200, 203-204, 207-210, 213-214, 217-218, 224-227, 232-234, 237, 239-241, 245-246, 267-268, 273-274, 278-279, 282, 307, 326, 328, 330, 334, 337

Gronkowski, Rob 38, 124, 126-127, 133, 136, 140, 143, 148-149, 153, 155, 183, 195-197, 211-212, 214-216, 220, 226, 228-229, 232, 240, 242-243, 247, 270, 280-281, 284, 295, 298-299, 301, 303, 326

H

Hail Mary Pass, 9, 126, 197, 218, 227, 240
Hal Stern, 147
Hall of Fame, 16, 27, 29, 35, 64, 67, 138, 145, 235, 249, 254, 296
Handicap, 63-64, 310
Handicapping, 137
Hard Rock Stadium, 33
Harris Poll, 25
Hedge bets, 89, 299
Hedging out, 145, 156, 201
Highest passer rating in a super bowl, 67, 254
Home field advantage, 6, 10, 73-75, 79-81, 84, 87, 96, 98-99, 101, 106-107, 116, 132, 136, 138-139, 142, 158, 179, 190, 220, 241, 267, 275, 280
Houston Texans, 20, 39, 46, 83, 105, 107, 116-118, 121, 128-129, 132, 137, 139-140, 143-144, 160, 183, 195, 217, 223-224, 233-234, 236-237, 241-243, 246-247, 249, 268-269, 273-274, 278-279, 282, 285, 307, 324, 326-327
Hull, Blair 139

I

Impossible is routine, 298
Indianapolis Colts, 5, 13-15, 18, 29, 31, 69-73, 79-80, 89, 92, 98, 101, 103, 105, 107, 109, 116, 123, 137, 150, 155, 164-165, 167, 168, 172, 182-183, 186-187, 190-191, 194, 200-204, 210-212, 213, 217, 229, 231, 249, 268, 273-274, 278-279, 282, 284, 307, 322, 324, 326
Information and beliefs, 90
Injuries, 6, 11, 19, 23, 83, 98, 193, 203, 214, 220, 226, 228, 233, 238, 266, 268, 272, 285, 321, 326-327, 335
Instant Replay, 22-23, 26
Intercepted, 61, 68, 76, 81, 98, 133, 143, 151, 173-174, 196, 198, 201, 207, 209, 211, 226, 238, 250-251, 277, 281

Interception, 61, 66, 68, 104, 126, 141, 143-144, 146, 149, 151-152, 155, 166, 171, 173, 190, 192, 196-197, 199, 201, 207-208, 212, 214-216, 228, 230-231, 238, 240, 244-246, 248, 252, 272, 284-285, 302, 304, 321, 329

J

Jacksonville Jaguars, 42, 76, 84, 105, 107, 116, 204, 268, 271, 273-274, 278-279, 282-284, 294-295, 297-299, 307, 334kn337
Jaguars, see Jacksonville Jaguars
James-Stein estimation, 82
Jet lag effect, 74, 267
Jets, see New York Jets

K

Kansas City Chiefs 18, 32, 42, 74, 101, 103, 105, 107, 116, 138, 163-165, 167, 183, 204, 217-218, 220, 223-224, 226, 233-234, 237-238, 240-241, 243-244, 247, 266, 268-270, 273-274, 278-280, 282, 284, 297, 324, 327, 334
Kelly criterion bets, 116
Kelly Handbook, 117
Kickers, 7
Kickoff return, 143

L

LA Chargers, 25, 33, 167, 204,, 267. 273-274, 278-280, 282, 284, 307, 334
LA Rams, 14-15, 22, 27-28, 33, 204, 235, 249, 268, 273-274, 276, 278-279, 281-284, 297, 307, 334
LA Stadium complex, 33
Lambeau field, 132
Las Vegas odds, 6, 10, 180, 182, 213, 334
Lead changes, 6, 91, 131, 296
League ranks:
passing, 331
rushing, 331
Legion of boom, 197, 224, 245, 328, 334

Linebackers, 7, 19, 52
Lions, see Detroit Lions
Logistic curve, 75, 86
Logistic model, 48, 51, 56, 320
Logit, 47, 61
Lombardi, 14, 16-17, 31, 37, 176, 304
Longshots, 79, 92, 257
Loss aversion, 92
Louisiana Superdome, 22, 28
Lynch, Marshawn 76, 91, 170-171, 173,
    175, 190, 195, 198, 207-210, 213-
    217, 221, 233, 239, 251, 270, 272,
    276-277, 284, 286, 329-330, 332, 334

M
MacLean, Leonard 5-6, 11, 69, 117,
    241, 252
Manning, Peyton 5, 29-31, 67, 69-71,
    81, 86, 92, 98-99, 109, 117, 123-
    124, 126-127, 132, 137, 140, 143-
    144, 149-150, 153, 155-156, 167, 169-
    170, 172-176, 182, 185, 191, 201-
    202, 210, 217, 220, 228-230, 233,
    237, 239-240, 249, 254, 267, 270,
    274-275, 280
Margin of Victory Multiplier, 85
Margin, 63-64, 84-85, 179, 231
Marginal probabilities, 62
Mean reversion risk arbitrage, 10-11,
    83, 126, 141, 209, 216, 288, 294
Mean reversion, 6, 10-11, 70, 74, 82-
    83, 89-91, 124, 126-127, 131, 135,
    140-141, 145, 150, 165, 172, 180,
    189, 209, 216, 221, 227, 250, 266,
    271, 288, 294, 296, 303
    regression toward the mean, 82
Mercedes-Benz Stadium, 33
Miami Dolphins, 18, 19, 21-22, 24-26,
    30, 32-33, 79, 96, 105, 107, 112,
    116, 163, 183, 204, 220, 231, 233-
    234, 236-238, 240, 249, 273, 278-
    279, 282-284, 286, 294, 302, 326,
    334
Minnesota Vikings, 18, 20-21, 26, 33,
    80, 87, 98-99, 105, 107, 116, 137,
    204, 217-218, 224-225, 232, 257, 268,
273-274, 278-279, 282-283, 294, 296-
297, 299-301, 307, 324, 327, 330,
334, 337
Model Predictions, 53-54
Monday Night Football, 8
Morris, Benjamin 193
Multiple linear regression, 51
MVP, 31, 36, 69-70, 92, 102, 127, 137,
    141, 153, 155, 172, 176, 180, 185,
    199, 202, 216, 218, 220-221, 224,
    228-230, 232, 238, 242, 249, 252,
    267, 270, 274-276, 280, 294, 299,
    301, 304, 321, 326

N
National Conference, 95, 136
New coaches, 321-322
New England Patriots, 5-6, 10, 16, 22,
    24, 28-29, 31-32, 35-36, 42, 52-53,
    69-73, 76, 78, 80, 83-84, 91, 101-
    105, 107, 109, 116-118, 123-129, 132-
    133, 136-140, 143-149, 152-153, 155,
    158-159, 164, 167-171, 179-180, 182-
    183, 185-187, 190-191, 194-197, 201,
    203-204, 210-218, 220-221, 224, 226,
    228, 230-234, 237, 239-244, 246-252,
    254-255, 257, 267-268, 270–274, 276-
    285, 289, 294-295, 297-299, 301-304,
    307,322, 324, 326, 328-330, 334-35
New Orleans Saints, 6, 18, 28, 31, 79-
    81, 89-91, 98-99, 101, 103, 105, 107-
    109, 111, 116-118, 121, 123, 128-
    132, 135, 153, 156, 158, 163-164,
    166-168, 183, 185, 191, 204, 249,
    267-268, 271, 273-274, 277-279, 282,
    285, 294, 296-297, 307, 324, 326,
    330, 334, 337
New York Giants, 13, 15-16, 18, 24, 28,
    30-31, 80, 84, 105, 107, 112, 116-
    118, 123-129, 132, 139, 187, 195,
    204, 218, 221, 233-234, 237, 239-
    240, 245-246, 249, 257, 267-270, 273-
    275, 278-280, 282, 298, 307, 324,
    326, 334
New York Jets, 16-18, 29, 32, 83, 101,
    103-105, 107, 112, 116, 130, 204,

218, 272-274, 278-279, 282, 284, 334
NFC championship, 96, 136, 200, 229,
    277, 296, 299
NFL championship bets, 145
NFL Draft, 11, 25, 275, 337, 346, 348
NFL Europe League, 26
NFL football betting market, 135
NFL Management, 19, 25
NFL Network, 29
NFL Players Association, 14, 19, 25
NFL protests, 138
NFL Top 100, 42, 44
Normal distribution, 23, 63-64
    cumulative normal distribution, 64
NY Giants, see New York Giants

O

Oakland Raiders, 16, 18, 21,2 3- 24,
    29, 31-32, 64, 73-74, 105, 107-108,
    112, 116, 130, 153, 204, 220-221,
    232-237, 249, 266, 268, 270-274, 276,
    278-279, 281-282, 284-286, , 322,
    324, 332, 334
Odds favorite, 112, 124
Odds of winning, 5, 10, 61-62, 64, 71,
    75, 79, 83, 86-87, 96, 109, 124, 130,
    136, 158, 190-191, 194, 220, 294,
    306, 310, 329
Odds ratio, 47, 61-62
Offensive player of the year, 195, 249
Operational risk, 144
Order Preserving, 67
Osweiler, Brock 217, 220, 230
Over bet, 92, 127, 155
Over the point spread, 63
Overtime, 14, 18-19, 29, 77, 81, 92,
    98-99, 132-133, 144, 156, 210, 213,
    227, 252, 254, 270-271, 277

P

Packers, see Green Bay Packers
Panthers, see Carolina Panthers
Pass interference, 143, 151, 192, 216
Passer rating, 66-68, 253-254
Patricia, Matt, 322
Patriots, see New England Patriots,

Payton, Walter 20-22, 24, 26, 29, 175,
    249, 274
Performance Measures, 38, 64, 66
Philadelphia Eagles, 6, 10, 15, 18, 24-
    25, 31-32, 53, 76, 85, 101, 103, 105,
    107-108, 116, 156, 158, 163-164, 166,
    182-183, 185, 204, 268, 272-275, 278-
    280, 282-283, 285-286, 294, 296-297,
    299-304, 307, 324, 326-327, 334-335
Pinnacle, 6, 176, 242, 294, 296, 300
Pittsburgh Steelers, 14, 18-19, 21, 23,
    28-29, 31, 35-36, 42, 76, 92, 101-
    103, 105, 107-108, 118, 121, 123,
    129, 132-133, 163, 176, 180, 182,
    186-187, 190, 194-195, 204, 218, 221,
    223-224, 227, 232-234, 237-238, 241,
    243-244, 247-248, 268, 273-274, 278-
    283, 285, 294-297, 299, 307, 328,
    334, 337
Play of the year, 195, 249
Player ratings, 36
    100 greatest current players, 38
Players under suspension, 326
Playoff picture, 284, 291
Playoff tree, 98, 137, 164, 187, 224
Pocket, 124, 207, 220
Point Spread, 11, 62-64, 83-84, 112,
    124, 130, 147, 176-177, 310, 313
Power Index, 83, 335
Predicting win probabilities, 305, 307,
    309, 311, 313, 315, 317, 319
Prediction accuracy, 74
Predictions, 9-11, 53-54, 82, 102, 109,
    182, 241, 249, 257, 259, 261, 263,
    265, 267, 269, 271, 273, 275, 277,
    281, 283, 285, 287, 289, 318, 320
Pro Bowl, 25, 146, 167, 170, 196, 218,
    277, 332
Pro Football Hall of Fame, 16, 29, 67,
    254
Probabilities of winning, 64, 86, 96,
    109, 136, 194
Probability, 47, 59, 61-62, 64, 71-73,
    75, 83-84, 86, 93, 110, 116, 124,
    158, 214, 305-306, 310, 320, 329

Q

Quarterback ratings, 10, 66, 68-69, 156, 235, 240, 253, 274, 321-322, 324
Quarterback sneak, 76, 124
Quarterbacks, 5, 7-9, 19, 31, 68-69, 123-124, 127, 137-138, 150, 176, 182, 196, 200-201, 210, 221, 231-232, 236, 242, 249, 266, 271, 275, 337

R

Racetrack betting, 92, 180
Raiders, see Oakland Raiders
Rams, see LA Rams
Ravens, see Baltimore Ravens
Record against the spread, 194
Redskins, see Washington Redskins
Riggle, Rob, 322
Risk arbitrage bettors, 130
Risk arbitrage, 6, 10-11, 74, 83, 89-91, 124-131, 133, 135, 141, 173, 180, 189, 201, 209, 216, 280, 288, 294, 298, 300
Robbe, Joe 33
Rodgers, Aaron, 38, 67, 83, 102, 109, 117, 102, 123, 166, 180, 182, 191, 194, 199-200, 207-210, 218, 225-227, 231-232, 235-236, 239-240, 245-246, 248-249, 254, 276, 326
Romer analysis, 71
Romo, T., 191-193, 195, 199-200, 233, 337
Rookie of the year, 137, 195, 249
Roughing the passer, 25, 98, 201, 208
Runline, 176
Running backs, 7-8, 19, 156, 167, 212, 300
Rushing statistics, 67, 254

S

Saints, see New Orleans Saints
San Diego Chargers, 25
San Francisco 49ers, 6, 14, 23-28, 30, 32, 35, 64, 90-91, 105, 107-108, 111, 116-118, 123-124, 128-132, 136-141, 143-147, 149-153, 155-156, 158, 164, 166-171, 174, 182, 204, 251, 273-274, 277-279, 282, 324, 326, 328, 330
Scrambler, 151, 167, 295
Seahawks, see Seattle Seahawks
Seattle Seahawks, 26, 29-32, 42, 46, 74, 76, 83, 91, 101, 103, 105, 107, 136-139, 142-144, 146, 156, 158-160, 163-164, 167-177, 179, 181-183, 185-187, 190-191, 193-195, 197-201, 203-04, 207-210, 212-217, 220-221, 224-225, 227, 229, 232-234, 237-239, 244-249, 251, 267-268, 272-279, 281-282, 284-285, 321-322, 326-335, 337
record by year, 330
starters, 333
Segmented global market, 176
Shorting, 139, 149, 194, 201, 215
Silver, Nate 82, 179, 194, 201, 220
Smart money, 213
Sports betting, 10, 69, 89-90, 96, 310
Sports Illustrated, 5, 9, 36, 38, 42-43, 46-47, 55, 57, 257
Spread betting, 63, 310
Spreads, 5, 10, 82-83, 89, 109, 115, 179, 186, 201, 288, 305, 307, 309-311, 313, 315, 317, 319
Stadiums, 28, 33, 91, 107, 130, 132, 152, 156, 167, 172, 175, 229, 235, 257, 270, 283, 301, 337
Statistics, 5, 59, 62, 64, 67-69, 71, 149, 160-161, 187, 241, 248, 252-254, 331, 335
Steelers, see Pittsburgh Steelers
Stochastic process, 89
Suggs, T, 39, 190
Super Bowl 50, 277
Super Bowl 51, 91, 254, 257, 266
Super bowl 52, 6, 8, 10, 53, 83, 257, 301, 335
Super Bowl bets, 115, 138, 140, 158, 168, 170, 207, 210, 213, 216, 218, 243, 248
Super Bowl combo, 159, 169
Super Bowl MVP, 127, 155, 252, 274
Swetye, see Elo

T

Take-Aways, 161

Tampa Bay Buccaneers, 31-32, 42, 105, 107-108, 116, 204, 233, 249, 272-274, 278-279, 282, 307, 322, 324, 334

Team composition, 35, 37, 39, 41-43, 45, 47, 49, 51, 53, 55, 57, 305

Team rank, 305, 309, 331

Team statistics, 331

Team Strength, 79, 305, 307

Tebow, Tim 92, 132-133

Tebowing, 132

Tennessee Oilers, 26

Tennessee Titans, 26, 28, 105, 107, 116, 204, 221, 268, 273-274, 278-279, 282-284, 294-295, 297, 322, 324, 334

Texans, see Houston Texans

Three-peat, 139

Time outs, 70, 142, 144, 147, 151, 210

Titans, see Tennessee Titans

Tom Cover, 59, 253

Top players, 38, 42, 46-48, 50-51, 57, 332

Top seed, 96, 136, 239

Total offense, 160, 232

Turn-of-the-year effect, 125

Turnover statistics, 160

Two versus one extra point fallacy, 77

Two-stage modeling, 72

U

UK odds, 90, 92, 135

Undefeated season, 79, 228

Underdog, 62-63, 73, 84, 89, 130, 141, 153, 177, 190, 267, 271, 275, 310

Upset, 80, 87, 99, 123, 140, 283

US Bank Stadium, 33, 257, 301

US football markets, 135

US odds, 90, 92, 135

Utility function, 72

V

Vikings, see Minnesota Vikings

Vince Lombardi trophy, 176, 304

Vrabel, M, 70, 322

W

Walter Payton Man of the Year, 26, 274

Washington Redskins, 21-22, 24, 26, 28, 91, 105, 107-108, 116, 137, 142, 204, 217, 220, 224-225, 234, 241, 271, 273-274, 279, 282, 330, 324, 327

Watt, JJ. 38, 46, 195-196, 218, 236, 242, 268, 285, 326

Weighting by position, 48

Welker, Wes, 104, 133, 143, 148, 155, 167, 170, 173-175, 201

Wentz, Wes 36, 272, 275-276, 280, 285, 294, 300, 302, 321-322, 326-327

Wide receivers, 7-8, 19-20, 138

Wild card, 18-19, 25, 96, 99, 118, 132, 136-137, 139-140, 156, 164, 183, 187, 189, 206, 223-224, 233, 237, 248, 277, 284, 297, 330,

Wildcard weekend, 91, 117, 120-121, 127, 156, 158, 163, 165, 193, 236

Wilson, Russell, 17, 20, 39, 46, 76, 91, 137, 142-143, 156, 170-173, 175-176, 182, 195, 197-199, 207-210, 213-216, 218, 220-221, 224, 226-227, 229, 233, 239, 244-245, 251, 267, 272, 275-277, 284-285, 294, 329, 332, 334

Win percentage, 36, 42, 46-47, 51, 57, 193

Win probabilities, 82, 305, 307, 309, 311, 313, 315, 317, 319

Work the position, 131

Z

Ziemba, William T, 5-6, 10-11, 48, 68-69, 74, 80, 89-94, 99, 117, 135, 138, 147, 153

CPSIA information can be obtained
at www.ICGtesting.com
Printed in the USA
BVHW05s1841080918
526661BV00001BB/4/P